D1490531

JOHN SHEIR
DEC, 25/10

GREAT PASS RECEIVERS OF THE NFL

Exciting profiles of eleven famous NFL ends and backs whose sure-handed pass-catching made them stars. They are Mike Ditka, Pete Retzlaff, Del Shofner, Bobby Mitchell, Dave Parks, Bob Hayes, Mac Speedie, Dante Lavelli, Jimmy Orr, Bill Howton and Don Hutson.

GREAT

Random House · New York

PASS
RECEIVERS
OF
THE
NFL

by Dave Anderson
Illustrated with photographs

© Copyright, 1966, by Random House, Inc.

All rights reserved under International and Pan-American Copyright Conventions. Published in New York by Random House, Inc., and simultaneously in Toronto, Canada, by Random House of Canada Limited.

Library of Congress Catalog Card Number: 66-10695

Manufactured in the United States of America

Introduction

The pass is perhaps the most exciting play in pro football. As talented as the passers themselves are, their ability would be wasted without the players who catch the ball.

Several factors are necessary for a player to be a great pass receiver. He must have good hands because if he can't hold onto the ball, he is worthless. He must have the speed to get downfield quickly. He must have the moves or the fakes which fool the defensive back covering him. He must have the timing to break into the clear at the precise moment when the ball is coming at him. He must have the strength and the courage to fight for the ball, to "catch it in a crowd," as the coaches say. He must have the ability to escape for more yardage *after* catching the ball. He must have an intellectual rapport with his passer. Finally, he must be durable, because he is subject to some of the most bone-crushing tackles in the game.

Years ago a pass receiver was, simply, an end. But in today's more complex offensive formations, pass receivers perform at three positions: flankerback, split end and tight end. The flankerback is actually the right halfback. He lines up a yard behind the line of scrimmage 15 or 20 yards from the quarterback, usually to the right side of the field. The split end is usually on the left side. He lines up on the line about 10 or 15 yards away from the left tackle. The tight end lines up next to the tackle, usually on the right side. In addition to receiving passes, he is used as a blocking lineman on running plays. Sometimes the flankerbacks and split ends are interchanged by coaches. But a tight end remains in the offensive line.

With the development of the forward pass as football's most potent weapon, pass receivers have developed into high-salaried stars. Clearing the way for them was Don Hutson, the first of the prolific pass receivers who played several decades ago with the Green Bay Packers. Hutson, of course, is included in this volume along with three other now retired performers: Bill Howton, Dante Lavelli and Mac Speedie. Several current stars are included: Mike Ditka, Bobby Mitchell, Pete Retzlaff, Jimmy Orr, Del Shofner, Dave Parks and former Olympic sprint champion Bob Hayes.

Four other famous pass receivers—Raymond Berry, Tommy McDonald, Frank Gifford and Elroy Hirsch— appear in another volume of The Punt, Pass and Kick Library, *Heroes of the NFL*.

The pass receivers in this book have become some of the most spectacular players in the National Football League. The next time you see a pass completion, remember to give credit not only to the passer, but to the pass receiver. If *he* hadn't caught it, there would not have been a completion.

Contents

GREAT PASS RECEIVERS OF THE NFL

1

Mike Ditka

Up on the scoreboard, the final minutes were ticking away. The Chicago Bears were losing to the Pittsburgh Steelers, 17–14, in this late-season 1963 game at Pitt Stadium. The Bears and the Green Bay Packers were battling for the Western Division lead. If the Bears lost to the Steelers, they would drop into second place behind the Packers. They needed a tie, at least, but they were on their own 22-yard line in an almost hopeless situation. It was third down and 33 yards to go for a first down.

In the huddle quarterback Bill Wade called the play. As the huddle broke, the Bears clapped their hands and trotted to the line of scrimmage. Mike

Ditka, a big "89" on his Bear jersey, lined up at tight end. In most pro formations, there is a tight end who lines up next to his tackle and a split end who lines up several yards wide of his tackle. At the snap, quarterback Wade spun and moved back into the protective pocket formed by his pass blockers. Wade didn't wait long. He saw Ditka moving across the middle, and he threw.

Ditka caught the ball a few yards downfield. He was being covered by Steeler safety man Clendon Thomas. As Ditka turned to run with the ball, Thomas tackled him low. For a split second, Ditka appeared to be stopped. But he shook his massive six-foot three-inch, 230-pound frame and broke the tackle. He spun away and moved upfield. Three other Steelers converged on him. Then a fourth and a fifth. Somehow Ditka's tree-trunk legs continued to churn. One by one, the Steeler players sprawled in his wake. At midfield he was suddenly in the clear. But he was weary. He stumbled into Steeler territory and made the first down. He went to the 15-yard line before Clendon Thomas, the first Steeler he had shaken off, caught him and dragged him down. As he explained later, "My legs were cramped up. I knew I'd be caught, but I figured I'd go as far as I could."

Moments later Roger Leclerc kicked an 18-yard

field goal. The game ended in a 17–17 tie. The Bears stayed in first place and went on to win the National Football League championship. George Halas, the elderly coach known as Papa Bear, admitted, "Ditka's play in Pittsburgh saved our season."

"The way Mike blasted through those tacklers," quarterback Bill Wade said, "was unbelievable. It was one of the greatest runs I've ever seen." Wade has seen many runs during his ten years in the NFL. But it is typical of Mike Ditka's style as a pass receiver that his performance against the Steelers is remembered for what he accomplished *after* he caught the ball.

Unlike split ends and flankerbacks, Ditka does not depend on speed. As a tight end, he must be a good blocker as well as a pass receiver. On a running play, he is responsible for blocking the outside linebacker, who is often one of the toughest men on the defensive team. When he does run a pass pattern, Ditka must be powerful enough to slam past the linebacker, who will try to nail him as he comes off the line of scrimmage. When he catches the ball, he is usually surrounded by tacklers. The tight end's job is not only to catch the ball, but to get the first down, whether he needs two yards or twenty. He is a team's clutch receiver,

Always a good blocker, Mike here sets up a
touchdown for fellow pass receiver Johnny Morris
(47) by taking number 35 out of the play.

as Mike Ditka showed in that game in Pittsburgh.

A few weeks later, in the 1963 NFL championship game in Chicago, Ditka came through again.
This time the New York Giants were leading the
Bears 10–7. It was the third quarter. The Bears
had the ball on the Giant 12-yard line, third down
and nine. If they failed to make a first down on
this play, they would have to settle for a field-goal
attempt. All afternoon the round-faced, crew-cut
Ditka had been trying to convince Billy Wade to
call the Look-In pass—the one in which Ditka cuts
to the inside and catches the pass over his inside
shoulder.

"The Look-In will work," Ditka kept telling the
coaches on the sidelines. "Their linebacker doesn't
touch me."

The coaches didn't seem to be listening. They
ignored Mike's suggestion. But now, as the Bears
prepared to go into the huddle before this crucial
third-down play, a substitute guard ran in from
the sidelines.

"The Look-In pass to Mike," the sub told Wade.

At the snap Ditka broke by the Giant linebacker
and slanted across the middle. Wade put the pass
right into his hands. Ditka caught it and burst by
the Giant defensive back assigned to cover him.
Another Giant pulled him down on the one. First

7

down. Moments later Wade scored on a quarterback sneak. The Bears led, 14–10. Neither team scored again, and the Bears had won the championship.

Mike Ditka is like all pass receivers. When he is in the clear, he *expects* to have the ball thrown to him. But he plays for the glory of the Chicago Bears, not for the glory of Mike Ditka. In a 1963 game against the Los Angeles Rams, the Bears had a big lead. The reason for the big lead was that Ditka had caught four touchdown passes. Another touchdown catch would set a Bear record.

"Anybody else would have come to me and said, 'I need one more,'" said Rudy Bukich, the Bear quarterback that day. "But Mike never mentioned it to me."

Another thing Mike Ditka doesn't mention is injuries. In 1964 he suffered a dislocated left shoulder during the College All-Star Game. He had to wear a leather brace all season. Every time he was tackled or lifted his arm to make a catch, the pain would shoot through his shoulder. But despite the pain, he caught 75 passes for 897 yards and five touchdowns.

In 1965 the shoulder had healed, but early in training camp Mike tore ligaments in his right foot. The doctor told him that some of the torn ligaments were under his arch, causing the arch to drop. It was a painful injury and could only be cured by staying off the foot until it healed. Mike agreed to rest the foot as much as possible, but he insisted that when the season opened he would play whether the foot healed or not.

When the season opened, the foot had not healed. But Mike played anyway. "Every step, I get a lot of pain on it," he admitted at the time, "but I try to forget it. I'm paid to play. That means whether I'm hurt or not. If you're a receiver, you've got to think about making your cut and beating the defensive back. You don't have time to think about your foot hurting, too."

The other teams knew that Ditka's right foot was sensitive. In a game in Los Angeles early in the 1965 season, Ditka went down in a pile-up. One of the Ram tacklers grabbed Ditka's foot and twisted it. Mike made a mental note of which Ram had done it. Then he got up, and trying to hide his limp, he went back to the huddle for the next play. "I know who it was," he said later. "It'll even out some day."

While Ditka patiently waited for a chance to even that score, he continued to catch passes. During his first five seasons with the Bears, he caught 284 passes, far more than any other NFL tight end

9

in that time. In each of those five seasons Ditka was selected to the Western Division All-Star team which played in the post season Pro Bowl. In 1961 he was voted the Rookie of the Year. He has been a consistent All-NFL choice.

As a boy, Mike Ditka never dreamed of such a celebrated career. He was born Michael Keller Dyzcko on October 18, 1939, in the steel-mill town of Carnegie, Pennsylvania, not far from Pittsburgh. Dyzcko is a Ukrainian name pronounced *Dish-ko.* Rather than pronounce it properly, however, neighbors called Mike and his two younger brothers "the Ditka kids." Mike's father finally changed the spelling of the family name to "Ditka."

But his father couldn't do much about Mike's size. When he entered nearby Aliquippa High School, Mike was a skinny five feet six inches tall. He weighed only 118 pounds. He wanted to play football, but the first day of practice he was one of the smallest boys on the squad.

Day after day he took a physical beating. After a few weeks of it, he came home one evening tired and discouraged. "I'm gonna quit the team," he told his parents. "I'm too small. The other guys beat me up every day."

His parents changed his mind. They encouraged

him to stay on the team. They promised to buy him health foods and suggested he start a daily program of calisthenics. The health foods helped. Mike ate spoonfuls of wheat germ with his meals. He gulped vitamin pills. The calisthenics developed his muscles. Every day he did 25 push-ups and 25 sit-ups. In later years he once did 55 consecutive finger-tip push-ups. By his senior year in high school, he had filled out to a lean, hard 185 pounds.

He also had learned from Coach Aschman what football was all about. "He taught me that desire is the big thing," Mike recalls. "Whenever I get a letter from a kid who tells me how big and fast he is, I write back and tell him that's fine but desire is more important. The most important thing about football is to want to play, to try. That's desire."

Ditka displayed his desire as a fullback on offense and as a linebacker on defense at Aliquippa High. Going on to the University of Pittsburgh, where he was a pre-dental student, he was moved to offensive end. He had played end briefly at Aliquippa, and he knew the fundamentals. But at Pitt his reputation was based mostly on his bruising defensive play as a linebacker.

In a game against Army, he ran 45 yards downfield on a pass pattern. But the pass was intercepted by one of the Cadet defensive halfbacks. Hoping

11

to tackle him, Ditka whirled and flung himself at the Army player. He missed. Instead of watching the Army player run, Ditka scrambled to his feet and chased after him. He caught him at the original line of scrimmage, helping to preserve a 7–7 tie. On this one play, he ran about 90 yards at top speed. He was momentarily exhausted and had to be helped from the field.

"Mike Ditka," said his Pitt coach, John Michelosen, "has more gung-ho in him than any player I ever had."

This gung-ho attitude—"gung-ho" is the battle cry of the U.S. Marine Corps—was evident throughout Ditka's college career. One day during his junior season, he was annoyed at the lackadaisical performance of his teammates in practice. They were about to play Syracuse. Coming off the field, he grumbled to a newsman, "If we play like this Saturday, we'll lose by 50–0."

When the quote appeared in the newspaper the next day, the Pitt coaches were furious. "But I wasn't too far wrong," Mike told a friend later. "We got beat by 35–0."

The next year, Ditka was the Pitt captain. Before the Syracuse game, he called a private meeting of his teammates. No coaches were permitted. "We're

12

not going to get beat again like last year," Mike growled. "Anybody who doesn't have the desire will answer to me."

Inspired by Ditka's words, or by his threat, the Pitt players not only won in an upset, they ended Syracuse's 17–game winning streak. Mike Ditka's performance earned him Lineman of the Week honors from *The Associated Press*.

Several weeks later Mike was selected on almost every All-America team. The All-America honors pleased him, but they did not impress him. "I knew that All-America doesn't mean a thing in pro football," he said later.

Ditka meant plenty to the pros. His hometown Pittsburgh Steelers hoped to draft him. But the Steelers had traded away their first four draft choices. They had no chance to get him unless the other NFL teams ignored him through four rounds.

"Look, Mike," a Steeler representative said to him, "let it be known you only want to play in Pittsburgh."

Ditka refused. He knew that he might be picked in the *first* round, gaining a chance to earn more money and more notice. The Bears of the NFL and the Houston Oilers of the American Football League both picked him in the first round. The Oilers

13

offered him more money, but Mike decided to sign with the Bears. "I made up my mind to play in the best league," he explained, "and the NFL is the best."

As a rookie in the Bear training camp, he was placed at tight end by Coach Halas. This decision surprised people in Pittsburgh who had assumed Ditka would be a linebacker. But Halas had scouted films of Ditka. The old coach saw that he had been a bruising blocker in Pitt's predominantly running offense. He saw, too, that when Ditka went out for a pass, he caught it and then bowled over his tacklers. Halas decided to test Mike at tight end. It was a wise decision.

In his first exhibition game, Ditka caught a 12-yard pass for a first down. When he returned to the huddle, quarterback Bill Wade told him, "This time fake the short pattern and take off on a fly when the safety man comes up." Ditka executed the pattern perfectly and the pass clicked for a 70-yard touchdown.

Day by day, the Bear veterans began to realize that Mike was not only going to make the squad, but that he was going to move in as a regular at tight end. Joe Fortunato, the veteran Bear linebacker who covered Ditka in the daily drills, said that summer, "Most rookies are easy to handle.

Bear quarterback Rudy Bukich (10) completes
a pass to Ditka (89).

They don't know the tricks. But Mike's different. He can fake you in, and he can fake you out. He's pretty good."

For a veteran to call a rookie "pretty good" is a high compliment. But Ditka didn't take it that way. "What's pretty good?" Mike bristled when told about Fortunato's evaluation. "There's pretty good, good, real good and great. Pretty good puts me at the bottom."

During his career, he has had several squabbles with linebackers. His most famous feud has been with Ray Nitschke, the middle linebacker of the Green Bay Packers. Their feud began in a 1963 exhibition game. Ditka blocked Nitschke from the blind side. Nitschke believed Ditka had gone out of his way to knock him down. After the game Ditka was having dinner with a few other Bears and Packers, including Nitschke. During a lull in the conversation Nitschke glowered at the big Bear.

"Ditka," Nitschke said, "you're a dirty player, and I'm going to get you."

Mike thought Nitschke was kidding. "I don't even hold any more," he replied.

But Nitschke wasn't laughing. "I'm still going to get you," he said threateningly.

"Too bad you feel that way," Mike replied evenly, "but you'd better get me first."

"And suppose I don't?" Nitschke snapped.

"Then I'll get you first," Ditka replied.

Several weeks later, in the opening game of the season, Ditka was running a pass pattern when the ball was thrown to another Bear receiver. Ditka peeled off, looking for somebody to block. The nearest man was Ray Nitschke. Ditka nailed him. Nitschke was shaken up and had to leave the game. In the locker room later, newsmen surrounded Ditka.

"I threw a good, clean block on Nitschke," Mike said. "I have nothing against him, and I respect him as a player. But it's not going to keep me from doing my job. I'm not trying to hurt somebody. I'm too much concerned with keeping myself from getting hurt."

The next summer, in the College All-Star Game, Ditka suffered his dislocated shoulder. He didn't cry about it, although it appeared that he had a reason to. He had caught a pass and was fighting for an extra yard when three All-Star tacklers dragged him down. He had his left arm extended and he was about to hit the ground when a fourth All-Star jumped into the pile-up and crashed into Ditka's forearm. The blow popped his shoulder out of its socket.

After the game, Ditka was sitting on the trainer's

17

Ditka is thrown high in the air by Ram defenseman
Carver Shannon.

table with his left shoulder swathed in tape. He had no complaints. "That guy who hit me last," Mike told the newsmen, "he had a right to do what he did. I was still trying to go forward. What if I had broken loose? Everybody would have told him he should have gotten me."

Ditka knows that pro football is a tough business, and he expects to take his punishment as well as give it out. He seldom complains and expects no complaints from others. Perhaps this is why the Bears respect him so much. He has been appointed captain of the Bears' offensive unit, by canny old Coach Halas, an unusual honor for a pass receiver, but a deserved one.

As Bear quarterback Rudy Bukich says, "Ditka is a leader. He's for the team 100 per cent. He drags you along with him."

2

Don Hutson

One day in the summer of 1961 some of the Green Bay Packer players were sitting around their locker room after a training camp workout. Their lanky pass receiver, Boyd Dowler, had made several spectacular catches in the passing drill, and his teammates were talking about his skill. Overhearing their conversation, the gray-haired team trainer, Carl "Bud" Jorgensen, spoke up with the experience of almost four decades with the Packers.

"Dowler is terrific," Bud Jorgensen said, "but if you think he's good, you fellows should have seen Don Hutson."

The Packer players knew of Don Hutson. But

21

he was someone out of the past. He began his National Football League career in 1935, when many of the current Packers had not yet been born. He retired after the 1945 season. The Packers knew he was great in his day. But some of them wondered out loud if Hutson would be as good if he were playing now.

"Well, let's see Hutson," star halfback Paul Hornung said. "There must be some of his game films around."

The next day Bud Jorgensen got out one of the old films. When the workout was over, he set up the movie screen and put the film in the projector. Hornung waited around to watch. So did Jesse Whittenton, an All-NFL defensive cornerback.

"Look at this," Hornung said, laughing.

On the screen Hutson was squatting in an old-fashioned stance.

"He's duck waddlin'," Whittenton said.

At the snap Hutson streaked down the field and made a move to his left. Three Chicago Bears were trying to stay with him. Hutson cut back to his right. Striding swiftly, he pulled away from all three Bears. He was alone when he caught the pass and pranced into the end zone for a touchdown.

"Run that over," Whittenton asked.

When he saw Hutson's moves and speed again, Whittenton shook his head.

22

"No one defensive back could cover that man," Whittenton admitted.

Hornung was shaking his head, too. "You just made a believer out of me," he said to Bud Jorgensen, who was smiling. "I've heard people argue what Hutson would do in this league if he were playing now. And I've wondered myself. Now I know. He'd do the same things he did when he was playing."

When Don Hutson was playing, he was the most feared pass receiver in pro football. Sleekly built at six feet one inch and weighing 178 pounds, Hutson set 19 NFL records while leading the Packers to three world championships. Many of his records still stand. In Hutson's years, most NFL teams were geared to a running offense. But he caught 488 passes for 7,991 yards. He scored 105 touchdowns. He even *threw* one touchdown pass. He led the league in pass receptions eight years. In addition, he was the Packer place kicker. He totaled 825 points. He won the NFL scoring championship five times. In 1963 he was elected one of the first members of the new National Pro Football Hall of Fame.

For all his records and honors, Don Hutson never boasted about them. He usually smiled shyly and said nothing. His actions spoke louder than

23

Not a man to give up easily, Hutson catches this
pass in spite of interference on his way to a
40-yard touchdown.

words, anyway. His actions, oddly enough, even contributed to the development of one of baseball's best players, Willie Mays. One day in 1964 Mays told how he is able to avoid crashing into the fence when chasing a long fly ball. "I learned to play fences by watching Don Hutson," Mays explained. "I saw him in the movies once. I watched the way he caught a football. He could catch it and stop real fast. I watched what he did. I said if he can do that with a football, why can't I do it with a baseball? Then I went out and ran hard at the fence and stopped. I kept doing it until I could do it well. He'd catch the ball and twist away from a guy going to tackle him. I catch the ball and twist away from the fence."

Perhaps Hutson's most memorable catch was made against the old Cleveland Rams. The Ram coach, Dutch Clark, assigned a halfback named Dante Magnani to cover Hutson. Clark did not believe that it was necessary to use two or sometimes three men to cover Hutson. Magnani was fast and he was tough. "Just one thing," Clark said to Magnani, "don't let Hutson get inside you."

Early in the game, Hutson moved down the field in low gear. Magnani was with him, stride for stride. Hutson shifted into second gear, and Magnani stayed beside him. Hutson looked around for

25

the pass. The Packer tailback, Tony Canadeo, had aimed it between the goalposts. Hutson went into high gear. Magnani was still with him as they dashed toward the goal posts. Then Hutson reached out, grabbed one of the goal posts with one hand and spun around.

He caught the pass for a touchdown. Magnani, as if he were covering a ghost, kept running through the end zone. Hutson had not planned this maneuver; he had done it instinctively. His instinct is what made him special. Nobody ever taught him how to feint defensive backs. He simply did it. Once Jock Sutherland, the coach of the old Brooklyn Dodgers, thought he had discovered a way to stop Hutson. But Hutson caught six passes that day, two for touchdowns, and the Packers won, 38–7. After the game, Sutherland said, "Hutson is incredible. He can run three ways at the same time."

Born on January 31, 1913, in Pine Bluff, Arkansas, a railroad town in the southeastern part of the state, Hutson was skinny and shy as a boy. He and his friend Bob Seawell enjoyed raising rattlesnakes, a hobby which did not exactly make them the most popular youngsters in town. When Seawell and Hutson weren't out in the hills chasing rattlesnakes, they were tossing a football or playing baseball. Seawell was the athletic hero of Pine Bluff.

In high school, Seawell talked Hutson into going out for the football team. Don made the team, but Bob remained the star. During their senior year, halfback Seawell was surrounded by recruiters from every leading college in the South. No one was interested in Hutson. Seawell selected the University of Alabama, on one condition. "If you want me," he told the man from Alabama, "you've got to take Don Hutson, too."

At the time Hutson weighed 145 pounds. He seemed too skinny to play football. But with his speed, the Alabama scout thought, maybe he could be a sprinter on the track team. Alabama agreed to Seawell's demand. But it didn't work out the way Alabama thought it would. By the end of his junior year, Seawell had dropped out of school, and Don Hutson had developed into an All-America end. His body had developed, too. He had grown to a wiry 175 pounds, but his increased weight had not affected his speed or his moves.

During his senior year he teamed with a strong-armed passer, Millard "Dixie" Howell. They formed a scoring combination which took Alabama all the way to the Rose Bowl. In addition to being a great pass receiver, Hutson was a tough tackler as a defensive back. And he played *without* shoulder pads because he gained more freedom of movement for catching passes.

The Crimson Tide's Rose Bowl opponent was powerful Stanford, led by tailback Bobby Grayson. But Hutson and Howell were too good. Alabama won 29–13, and Don attracted nationwide attention with his performance.

His most spectacular catch occurred on a play which was not supposed to be called. Hutson was relaxing on the bench late in the final quarter when Alabama coach Frank Thomas sent him into the game with orders for Howell to use running plays. The strategy, of course, was to run out the clock. But when Howell saw Hutson trotting onto the field, he assumed that Coach Thomas wanted him to go for a touchdown. Before Hutson could deliver his message, Howell called a pass play and the Alabama players hopped out of the huddle. Hutson ran his pass pattern and when he looked around, the ball was there. He caught it for a 56-yard touchdown.

Returning to the bench, Hutson explained to Coach Thomas what had happened in the huddle. With a grin, he added, "I had to catch that pass, Coach. It was too pretty to drop."

The Rose Bowl performance made Dixie Howell and Don Hutson famous. In the nation's newspapers they were compared to the famous passing combinations of the past. Hutson gave credit to Howell. On the train returning from the Rose Bowl to Alabama, Hutson sat by the window as the Texas prairies rolled by and told a newsman, "Dixie Howell is the greatest passer in the world. I run and break away and look over my shoulder and I say, 'Hello, football, I've been expecting you,' and then I catch it. I never worry about the ball. It never enters my mind. I know that when I look, the ball will be there. Howell throws a 'soft' ball. It's easy to catch."

Howell preferred to give credit to Hutson. "All I know is that Don catches them," he once said. "Throwing them isn't much. I guess the technique is timing. But it's more than that. It's knowing each other. I never worry about Hutson being there. I just throw the ball and he catches it."

The NFL coaches apparently agreed with Howell. They were much more interested in Hutson than they were in him. At the time there was no annual NFL draft of college players. As a result, Hutson was available to the highest bidder. During Alabama's regular season John "Shipwreck" Kelly, the

29

millionaire sportsman who owned the old Brooklyn (football) Dodgers, arrived on the Alabama campus to talk to Hutson.

"I agreed to sign with him," Hutson once said, "because he told me that he'd top any offer I got."

Several days before the Rose Bowl Game, however, Earl "Curly" Lambeau, the coach of the Green Bay Packers, arrived in California. He had made the trip specifically to see Hutson. The Alabama team was holding secret workouts. But one afternoon Lambeau scaled a wall and sneaked in to watch Hutson practice. One look was enough to convince him that Hutson was a potential pro star.

"He would glide downfield," Lambeau once recalled, "and he'd be leaning forward, as if to steady himself close to the ground. Then he'd feint one way, go the other, reach up like a dancer and gracefully squeeze the ball and leave the scene of the accident—the accident being the defensive backs who got their legs tangled up trying to cover him."

After Hutson's heroics in the Rose Bowl, Lambeau went after him. So did other NFL teams. "I was getting offers from everybody," Hutson has explained, "but Lambeau was really after me. With every offer, I would wire Kelly, and he'd wire me back saying the Dodgers would top the offer. It

30

All alone, Hutson goes after a pass from Arnold Herber in the 1938 championship game against the Giants.

wasn't like the big money the college players get now—with offers going up $10,000 at a time or anything like that. It was more like $10 a whack."

But Lambeau was using more than money. He was using psychology. "The Dodgers have no passer," Lambeau told Hutson. "At Green Bay we have one of the best passers in the league in Arnie Herber. The Dodgers don't use a passing attack. Their coach believes in a running offense. He likes big, strong players. You won't get the same opportunity that we'll give you in Green Bay."

Hutson sent a wire to "Shipwreck" Kelly, informing him of Lambeau's latest offer. This time there was no answer from Kelly. He sent another wire; no answer. A third wire; no answer. Don finally decided to accept the Green Bay contract. Several days later Kelly arrived at the Alabama campus. He had been in Florida and had not received any of Hutson's wires until, suddenly, he received all three of them at once. When Hutson told him about signing with the Packers, Kelly exploded.

"Hutson is my player," Kelly thundered at NFL Commissioner Joe Carr. "I want a ruling."

After an investigation, Carr decreed that Don Hutson was the property of the Packers. His decision may have saved Green Bay from losing its franchise. When the NFL was organized in 1920,

Green Bay was among its charter members along with several other small midwestern cities such as Decatur, Illinois, and Portsmouth, Ohio. The Decatur franchise soon shifted to Chicago, the Portsmouth franchise to Detroit. But the Packers not only survived in Green Bay, they thrived for many years. They won the NFL championship in 1929, 1930 and 1931. But then their reign was ended by the Bears.

The Packers had financial problems, too. The whole country was going through a depression, and many football fans couldn't afford to attend the games. Despite their hardships, the people of the small northern Wisconsin city rallied time and time again to keep the team in Green Bay. But by 1935, they were making their last stand. The residents had used their own money to form Green Bay Packers, Inc., in a desperate effort to save the team. Another poor season or two and the Packers probably would have had to move to a larger city.

But with Don Hutson, things were different for the Packers. Suddenly there was hope for a return to the glory years. The Green Bay fans knew this the first time they saw him. The Packers opened the 1935 season against the Bears. The Bears kicked off, and tailback Arnie Herber ran the ball out to the Packer 17-yard line.

Hutson waits for a pass during the championship 1944 season. He has outmaneuvered the defense again.

Coming out of the huddle, the Packers lined up in their single wing formation. Hutson was at left end. At the snap, the ball was centered to tailback Herber. He faked a handoff to the fullback and faded back to pass. Wingback Johnny "Blood" McNally, the veteran Packer star, raced downfield. Most of the Bear defensive backs were surrounding McNally.

Hutson, meanwhile, dashed past the Bear defender assigned to cover him. Herber let the ball go, and Hutson, gliding gracefully, caught it near midfield. Pounding along behind him was the fastest of the Bear defensive backs, Beattie Feathers. But Hutson ran away from him and coasted into the end zone. The skinny rookie had scored a touchdown on an 83-yard maneuver on his *first* play with the Packers. "I had a lot of thrills in pro football," Hutson once said, "but that first touchdown was the biggest of them all."

There were to be many more touchdowns as Hutson sparked the Packers to the NFL championship in 1937, 1939 and 1944. But he was more than a pass-catching specialist. He was an effective blocker, a sharp tackler as a defensive back and an almost perfect place kicker.

Off the field, Don Hutson was as shrewd as he was on it. He invested his Packer earnings wisely.

He became one of the leading businessmen in Racine, Wisconsin, not far from Green Bay. But every year the question faces the old NFL fans who saw Don Hutson, and the young NFL fans who wish they had seen him: would Don Hutson be as good now as he was then?

"That's a loaded question," Hutson always answers. "But I do know this—the defensive backs are better now because they only play defense. That makes a tremendous difference."

Then Hutson smiles and adds, "But a real good defensive back can't cover a real good receiver, man for man. If the receiver has time to maneuver, it's impossible to cover him."

It is impossible to be sure about Don Hutson's possible success under today's football conditions. But it's likely that defensive backs today wouldn't like covering him for an afternoon any more than the defensive backs of years ago.

3

Bobby Mitchell

The referee's whistle blew. "Official time-out," the voice droned on the public-address system in Cleveland's huge Municipal Stadium. "Two minutes to play."

Bobby Mitchell unclicked the chin strap on his burgundy helmet and took it off. He should have been frustrated and discouraged. Instead he held his head high. The previous four seasons he had played for the Cleveland Browns in the shadow of the famous fullback, Jim Brown. Now, on this sunny September afternoon in 1962, he had returned to Cleveland for the first time as a member of the Washington Redskins. He had been anxious to

39

play well, to show the Browns they had made a mistake in trading him.

But the Browns had geared their defense to stop Mitchell. Whenever he ran a pass pattern, the Browns used two and sometimes three men to cover him. The strategy was working. Mitchell, as he pointed out later, "had hardly touched the ball." The Redskins were losing, 16–10, but Bobby Mitchell was not losing his confidence.

"I knew they couldn't stop me the whole game," he said later in the dressing room. "There had to be one time for me."

The Redskins had the ball at the 50-yard line. They had been moving the ball with running plays. During the time-out, coach Bill McPeak told Redskin quarterback Norman Snead, "Now we pass. The next play, use the Halfback Flare with Bobby at halfback."

Snead nodded and trotted toward his teammates. In the huddle, he called "Halfback Flare," and Mitchell smiled. The play had been designed for him. Instead of being flanked out to the right as a wide receiver, he lined up in the running halfback's position, a few yards behind Snead. From this formation, Mitchell was to race downfield for a long pass. The Browns would have to use a linebacker to cover him. And there was no linebacker in the National Football League who could match Bobby Mitchell's speed.

At the snap Mitchell shot across the line of scrimmage. He was bumped by linebacker Galen Fiss and momentarily stunned, but he kept his feet. Unable to move downfield, he spun to the left. Snead, meanwhile, saw that Mitchell had been forced to break his pattern. With pass rushers swarming in, Snead drilled a short pass over the middle. Mitchell caught it. Squirming away from Fiss, he bolted toward the left sideline. "Somebody had a hand on me," Mitchell explained later. "He was angling on me, but I stopped and he shot past. Then there were the two safety men. But I went between them, *pfsst,* like that. And they didn't get me. Not today. Maybe some other day. But not today."

He dashed across the goal line for a touchdown. His "one time" had come. The Redskins won, 17–16. Mitchell had shown the Browns they had made a mistake. He had silenced the Cleveland crowd, too. After the game, the only noise in the ball park was in the Redskin dressing room where Mitchell's teammates hugged him, shook his hand and pounded him on the back. Leaning across his locker, he grinned.

"This was my greatest thrill," he said, "my

41

Mitchell flies past defenders on his way to the
50-yard touchdown that beat the Browns 17-16.

greatest everything. If I had become panicky or frustrated, it couldn't have happened. But I knew there had to be one time for me."

Later in the season, he explained, "It was an impossible run. I had nowhere to go, but I found somewhere. I don't think that many individuals could have done that. I don't think that I could do it again myself. It was the greatest run I've ever made, and I've made many a run, caught many a pass. And with all that pressure on me. That was confidence personified."

Some observers have complained that Mitchell is vain. His self-assurance has not always made him friends. But he says, "The worst guy in the world is the one who talks about what he's going to do and then does *not* do it. That is conceit. That is cockiness. But when a guy goes out and does what he says he's going to do, that's confidence."

Mitchell is blessed with sprinter's speed. But confidence is what has made him rank among the best pass receivers in NFL history. In the four seasons after the Redskins placed him at flanker-back, he caught more passes for more yards and more touchdowns than any other NFL receiver. His four-year totals were 261 receptions for 4,591 yards and 34 touchdowns. In 1962, he led the NFL with 72 receptions for 1,384 yards, the first flankerback

44

ever to do so. Bobby's confidence is supported by statistics.

As a senior at the University of Illinois, Mitchell was a sprinter on the track team. He could run the 100-yard dash in 9.5 seconds, but other American sprinters could run it faster. One day his coach, Leo Johnson, had a suggestion. "Bobby," the coach said, "why don't you try the hurdles? It'll lengthen your stride and help your football."

Mitchell agreed. As a hurdler, he had a new goal: to defeat Glenn Davis of Ohio State, the finest American hurdler. Davis had won the 400-meter hurdles in the 1956 Olympics, and he would win the event again in the 1960 Olympics. But Davis' reputation did not intimidate Mitchell.

When they met in a Big Ten track meet, Mitchell told Davis before the race, "I'm going to beat you." Davis only smiled and then defeated Mitchell. Then he defeated Mitchell in the next three meets. But on their fifth meeting, Mitchell not only beat Davis, he broke a world record for the 70-yard hurdles that had stood for 16 years. "And never again, did Davis ever touch me," Mitchell said later.

To Bobby Mitchell, the philosophy of confidence and determination applies off the field, too. Several years ago when he was playing in Cleveland, he phoned the president of a meat firm because he

Outrunning the defender, Mitchell snares a
touchdown pass against the Giants.

had decided that he could help the firm as a sales-
man. The president protested that he didn't need
any more salesmen.

"Do me a favor, sir," Mitchell replied. "Just let
me talk to you tomorrow at your office."

The president agreed, and the next day he
and Mitchell talked for an hour. When Mitchell
returned home, his wife Gwen, asked if he had been
hired. "Yes," Bobby said. "He didn't say so yet,
but I'm sure that I convinced him."

"Don't be silly," his wife said. "If he didn't say
anything, you have no chance at all." But that
evening, the phone rang. The company president
was calling to say he was putting Mitchell on the
payroll.

One of seven children, Robert Cornelius Mitchell
was born on June 6, 1935 at Hot Springs, Arkansas.
His father was a minister of the Church of God.
When he was a teenager, some of Bobby's friends
were getting into trouble with the police. "All of
a sudden," he said years later, "I was looking at the
other kids and thinking: I don't want to go where
they're going. I could see some of them were
headed straight for jail and that most of the rest
of them would never amount to anything. I made
up my mind I wouldn't be like them. So I had to

47

do better than them—in everything. If somebody was a fast runner, I had to be faster. If somebody hit a baseball far, I had to hit it farther."

He hit a baseball well enough to be offered a contract by the St. Louis Cardinals. But he turned it down to go to college. His heroics as a halfback in football and as a sprinter in track at Langston High School had earned him several college scholarship offers. He chose to attend the University of Illinois, where one of his buddies, Charles Butler, had enrolled the year before. As a sophomore, he was one of Illinois' regular halfbacks.

In his first game with the Illinois varsity, Mitchell ran 64 yards for a touchdown the first time he got the ball. Against Michigan he gained 173 yards in 10 carries. He set a Big Ten season record by gaining an average of 8.3 yards per carry. He appeared to have a sensational career ahead of him.

Two developments ended his dream of becoming an All-America halfback. As a junior he injured a leg and spent most of the season on the sidelines. As a senior, he had a reputation as a fumbler. The Illinois coach, Ray Eliot, described Mitchell as "a good running back who would be okay if you could teach him not to fumble." Eliot's diagnosis convinced most NFL scouts that Mitchell was a bad risk for a professional career.

But Paul Brown, then coaching the Cleveland Browns, had other ideas. One Saturday in 1957 he was watching the Illinois team in a televised game. Brown was greatly impressed by Mitchell's speed and balance and by his ability to stop and start almost instantly.

The day of the college draft, Brown had other players he preferred ahead of Mitchell. "But as I sat at the meeting," he recalled, "I kept wondering why nobody had drafted him. Finally I decided to pick him in the seventh round. It turned out to be the luckiest pick at that stage that I ever remember."

Several months later, Brown saw Mitchell in person for the first time. Bobby was in Cleveland for the Knights of Columbus Track Meet. When the meet officials called the contestants for the 50-yard dash, Mitchell strolled to the starting line and settled into a crouch. At the gun, he stumbled. But he regained his balance and qualified for the semifinals. In the next heat, he stumbled again at the start, but he came from behind to qualify. In the final, he got off flying and won in 5.3 seconds, tying a meet record. "Now there is an athlete," Paul Brown exclaimed while applauding Mitchell's victory.

But Mitchell was considering ignoring pro football offers. The 1960 Olympics were two years

49

away. Since he had beaten Glenn Davis, the 1956 hurdles champion, he thought he had a chance to win an Olympic gold medal as a hurdler. He was also competing in the broad jump. That spring he had scored 13 points by himself in leading Illinois to the Big Ten outdoor track championship and had qualified for the United States team which was to face Russia that summer.

As for football, he was discouraged by the criticism of his fumbling. But his wife, Gwen, whom he had met at Illinois, finally convinced him to try pro football.

One of Paul Brown's aides, Paul Bixler, came to the Illinois campus to talk about a Browns contract. Bixler made the mistake of asking Mitchell about his reputation for fumbling. "Don't talk to me about that," Bobby snapped. "The more they talk about it, the more tense I get."

Bixler changed the subject. He told Mitchell that the Browns needed a replacement for Ray Renfro, a veteran flanker who had suffered a knee injury the previous season. Renfro would have to test his knee before the Browns would know if he could stand up under NFL combat.

"If you want to use me at flanker, I'll sign," Mitchell told Bixler. "But I'm not big enough to be a running halfback."

Paul Brown, meanwhile, had looked at movies of Illinois games. "The films showed that the fumbles were not Bobby's fault," Brown said. "His team had several quarterbacks and the fumbles were caused mainly by bad ball handling by the quarterbacks, not by Bobby."

Brown decided to forget about the fumbles and sign Mitchell. He also asked Otto Graham, the former Brown quarterback who was coaching the College All-Star team, to put Mitchell on his squad. Graham agreed.

In the All-Star Game, Mitchell caught two touchdown passes in plays of 84 and 18 yards helping to upset the defending NFL champion Detroit Lions 35–19. He shared the Most Valuable Player award with quarterback Jim Ninowski of Michigan State, who had also signed a contract with the Browns.

But by the time Mitchell reported to the Browns training camp, Paul Brown had changed his mind about where to play him. Ray Renfro had recovered from his knee injury. He was set at flankerback. As a result, Mitchell would be tried at running halfback. He would also be employed to return kickoffs and punts.

In his first exhibition game with the Browns Mitchell stood on the goal line waiting to receive a kickoff. He reached for the ball, but it sailed through his hands. The fumbling hex had reappeared.

But Paul Brown didn't say a word, and slowly Mitchell relaxed. He was impressive enough at halfback to start the season next to fullback Jimmy Brown. Mitchell ran for 500 yards that season in only 80 carries for a remarkable average of 6.3 yards per carry. He scored six touchdowns—one as a runner, three as a pass receiver, one on a 98-yard kickoff return and one on a 68-yard punt return. In 1959 he ran for 743 yards and caught 35 passes for 351 yards. More and more, he was used as a pass receiver although his primary duty was running and blocking.

One day in 1960 Walt Yowarsky, scouting the Browns for the New York Giants, shook his head as he watched Mitchell. "He's the most dangerous and exciting player in pro football," Yowarsky said. "He can beat you by going 100 yards four different ways—taking a pass, returning a kick, going off tackle or turning an end. And he hasn't even reached his peak yet."

As it turned out, Mitchell would reach his peak with the Redskins rather than with the Browns. During the 1961 season Mitchell was inducted into the Army. He played on weekend leave and ran

Despite a determined Cardinal defender, Mitchell catches another touchdown pass.

for 548 yards. But Paul Brown had decided that Mitchell wasn't big enough to be a heavy-duty runner. He arranged a deal with the Redskins. Mitchell and halfback Leroy Jackson were traded for an option on All-America halfback Ernie Davis of Syracuse University. Tragically, Davis, the nation's outstanding college player in 1961, developed a fatal blood disease and died before he played even one game with the Browns.

Mitchell was soon installed as the Redskin flanker-back, the position he had always wanted to play. Suddenly he was a star with the Redskins, as he had never been with the Browns. In the 1962 season opener, he caught two touchdown passes and returned a kickoff 92 yards for another touchdown as the Redskins salvaged a spectacular 35–35 tie with the Dallas Cowboys. The next week, in Cleveland, he broke loose on the 50-yard touchdown play which he called "my greatest thrill, my greatest everything." More than any other player, he has been responsible for making the Redskins a championship contender once again. In each of the two previous seasons the Redskins had won only one game. But in 1962 they led the Eastern Division until the closing weeks of the schedule. Season by season, they have improved.

Mitchell's salary has improved too. The day he

joined the Redskins, owner George Preston Marshall told him, "You'll be a star here, but we don't have much money."

Mitchell nodded and smiled, remembering Marshall's reputation as a hard bargainer. But later that season, he told a luncheon group, "I hear we're selling tickets fast in Washington . . . I know there are people in those stands. Next year, I imagine, I'll be the highest paid man in pro football."

He never became the highest paid in the league, but by 1963 he was already the highest paid player in Redskin history. The Redskins were selling tickets fast, and people were buying them to see Bobby Mitchell.

4

Pete Retzlaff

One day in 1961 Sonny Jurgensen, the quarterback of the Philadelphia Eagles, emerged from his team's locker room at Franklin Field after a victory over the Pittsburgh Steelers. Nearby was Bobby Layne, the veteran Steeler quarterback. Layne stopped Jurgensen and said, "You know, Sonny, I've got your number on third down."

"What do you mean?" Jurgensen asked.

"When you need that first down," Layne said, "you go to Retzlaff every time."

Jurgensen smiled. He *did* prefer to throw to Pete Retzlaff when the Eagles needed long yardage for a first down. Jurgensen was not the only Eagle who relied on Retzlaff. In 1964 the Eagles had a new quarterback, Norman Snead. Snead soon developed the same pattern of throwing to Retzlaff in the clutch and has said, "Pete Retzlaff always seems to find a way to catch the ball."

Pete Retzlaff is blond and ruggedly handsome, and is a muscular six-feet one-inch tall. Entering the 1966 National Football League schedule, he had caught more passes than any receiver in Eagle history: 412 for 6,789 yards. At the age of 33, he had his finest season in 1965 with 66 receptions for 1,190 yards and 10 touchdowns. But he is more than a football player. He is one of the most respected and astute people in all of sports.

In addition to playing for the Eagles, he is a former president of the NFL Players Association, a radio and television sportscaster and a part-owner of a motel near Philadelphia. He has been chairman of the Teenage Committee of the March of Dimes in Philadelphia, co-chairman of the Athletes March on Hemophilia, co-director of the national Build Up Our Youth physical-fitness program and a trustee of the Pop Warner Ranch Hope for Boys.

Retzlaff's accomplishments have been recognized both in and out of football. He has been nominated for the National Junior Chamber of Commerce Young Man of the Year Award and was selected in 1965 as the Pro Football Father of the Year. He received a commendation from President Lyndon Johnson for his work in behalf of the J. D. Tippitt Fund, in honor of the Dallas, Texas, policeman who was slain by Lee Oswald following the assassination of President Kennedy.

"The busier I am," Pete Retzlaff says, "the more I seem to get done."

As busy as he is, he does not let anything interfere with his primary job: catching passes for the Eagles. One year a radio station wanted him to conduct post-game interviews each week from the Eagle locker room. But he turned the offer down. When asked for his reasons, he replied, "All I know is that at the end of a tight game, I don't want to be thinking about what I'm going to be talking about on a radio when the game's over. When I'm playing football, I've got to be thinking of only one thing: catching a pass when it's thrown to me."

"Let's face it," he once said, "my first responsibility is to the Eagles. If it hadn't been for my success with the Eagles, I would never have had an opportunity for the other things I do."

During his Eagle career, Retzlaff has shown himself to be not only loyal, but also unselfish and courageous. Late in the 1962 season, for example, Coach Nick Skorich needed a new tight end. The regular, Bobby Walston, was injured. One day after practice Skorich called Retzlaff aside.

"Pete," the coach said, "I'd like to use you at tight end from now on."

Retzlaff had established himself as one of the best split ends in the NFL. At split end he had more freedom to run pass patterns and was less likely to be injured. Tight end was a much more demanding position because of its blocking assignments and because the opposing linebackers lurk just across the line of scrimmage waiting for the tight end. Some players might have complained at the move. But not Pete.

Retzlaff played well in the final few games that season. Walston, the regular tight end, soon retired and Retzlaff continued as the tight end in 1963.

"On the outside as a split end," he has said, "I was primarily a receiver. I was concentrating 85 percent of the time on pass patterns. Playing the tight end, I'm a lineman, too. I have to throw blocks. I'm a factor in the running game. I no longer feel I'm a specialist. I'm more of a complete football player.

"At tight end I've got the linebacker standing over me, and I have to fight him for five or six yards to get free. Other times I have to block the defensive end or the linebacker. It would be sense-

60

Retzlaff (44) fights for a pass with a defender at the goal line.

less for me to try to overpower a 260-pound defensive end or a 230-pound linebacker. So I have to finesse them and sometimes that's not easy. Sometimes I line up on the right side, sometimes on the left. This means I've got to study two defensive ends, two linebackers and two safety men.

"When I was playing split end, I could go an entire half without knowing I'd accomplished anything. As a tight end, I'm involved in every play. It's more rewarding."

When Retzlaff moved to tight end, Mike Ditka of the Chicago Bears and Ron Kramer of the Green Bay Packers were rated as the best players in this position. But in 1965 Pete Retzlaff was selected to the All-NFL team. In proving his unselfishness in his willingness to change positions, he also proved his versatility.

Earlier, he had proved his courage. During an early season game in 1962 with the Cleveland Browns, the Eagles ran a play in which halfback Timmy Brown was to sweep Retzlaff's side. Retzlaff angled over to block middle linebacker Vince Costello. As Retzlaff lunged, his left forearm crashed against Costello's shoulder pad. This occurs often in every NFL game. But this time Retzlaff felt something snap, and he felt the pain shoot up his arm.

On the sideline Dr. James Nixon, the Eagle team physician, examined Retzlaff's arm. He suspected that Pete had broken a bone and urged that he go straight to the hospital for X rays. But Pete begged the doctor to put a temporary splint on the arm so that he could finish the game. The doctor finally agreed.

Retzlaff finished the game. That evening he went to the hospital for X rays. The photographs showed a fracture of the ulna bone in the forearm. Dr. Nixon announced that Retzlaff would be out of the lineup for eight weeks.

"Not me," Retzlaff said. "In 1959 I had a hairline fracture of my left leg, and I played in three or four weeks. I won't miss eight games."

He played two weeks earlier than the doctor had predicted. The fracture was not quite healed. But several days before he played, Dr. Nixon checked the arm and announced that barring another freak injury, there was no chance of another fracture.

Retzlaff played that Sunday with a light cast covered by sponge rubber. In order to protect the forearm as much as possible when tackled, he developed a habit of landing on his elbows. After the game, when he reported to Dr. Nixon for an examination of his arm, his elbow was purple. He had landed so often and so hard on the elbows that

63

Retzlaff is on his way down after catching a pass
against the Redskins.

he had broken some blood vessels. Soon Retzlaff's arm was purple from his wrist to his shoulder. But he kept playing.

"If you don't play in pain sometimes," he says, "you don't belong in this league."

When Palmer Edward Retzlaff was a boy, he thought that football was too rough. Born on August 21, 1932, in Ellendale, North Dakota, he grew up on his father's wheat farm with his older brother and two younger sisters. His mother, who had lived in Germany where soccer was a popular contact sport, considered football too rough for her sons. She forbade them to play.

Pete's older brother sneaked onto the Ellendale High School team without, he thought, his mother knowing it. And when Pete was 13, he went out for the team, too. But after a couple weeks of being battered and bumped by the varsity in practice scrimmages, he decided to quit. Thinking his mother would be pleased, he told her his plan to stop playing.

"I knew all the time you had gone against my wishes," she said. "For punishment, you now are going to have to keep playing."

This time Pete made the best of it. "If my mother had let me quit when I wanted to," he says now,

"I probably never would have played any more." He soon became a star high-school fullback with scholarship offers from such big-time football powers as Minnesota, Iowa and Nebraska.

But the big schools didn't impress him. "I went up to see the campus at Minnesota," he recalls, "and it was so big, I got lost." He decided to enter a smaller college instead: South Dakota State at Brookings.

At South Dakota State he set several school records as a fullback. In his senior season in 1952 he was named to the Little All-America team. In track and field, he competed in the shotput, the discus and the decathlon.

It seemed unlikely that he would be selected by an NFL team in the annual draft of college talent. In those days each team drafted 30 players. But scouting was not very thorough and Pete didn't have a big reputation.

One day he received a letter from the Chicago Bears. It informed him that if none of the NFL teams drafted him, the Bears would be interested in signing him as a free agent. But the Bears never had a chance. On the day of the draft the Detroit Lions selected him in the twenty-second round. The Lions obviously did not consider him a prize prospect. More than 250 players were picked ahead

67

of him. But they wanted to take a look at him, anyway.

At his first Lion training camp in 1953, Retzlaff was used at fullback. But the Lions, who had won the NFL championship the previous season, had several good runners. One day shortly before the season was to open, Coach Buddy Parker called Retzlaff into his office. "Pete," the coach said, "we want to put you on our taxi squad. We consider you an excellent prospect."

Rather than be a reserve player, Retzlaff decided to enter the Army. He had a two-year service obligation. When he returned he might have a better chance.

But when he returned to the Lions in 1956, the situation had not changed much. The Lions had all the runners they needed. He was switched to end, but the Lions also had several experienced pass receivers. Eventually he was placed on waivers, whereby any other NFL team could purchase his contract for $100. The next day a telegram arrived in the NFL office saying that the Philadelphia Eagles claimed Pete Retzlaff.

While Retzlaff was in the Army, he could have signed with the Eagles. Technically he was a free agent. He discovered that George Wilson, the Lions' assistant coach had told an Eagle assistant,

Charley Gauer, about him. "We can't use him," Wilson had said. "There are too many veterans ahead of him. But he might make it."

When the Eagles contacted him during his Army stint, Retzlaff rebuffed them. He preferred to try out with the Lions. But when the Lions put him on waivers and the Eagles claimed him, he was delighted to report. He made the team, but for two seasons he was used as a substitute, both as a running back and as a defensive back. One day in 1958 the new Eagle head coach, Buck Shaw, moved him to split end. Shaw had seen films of Retzlaff catching passes as a halfback.

"You have good hands," Shaw told him, "and you run well. Try it for a while and see how it goes."

It was one of Shaw's master moves. That season Retzlaff caught 56 passes to share the league lead with Raymond Berry of the Baltimore Colts. In 1960 he was a key player as the Eagles won the NFL championship. He was a star now, but because of his Army service and two unproductive seasons as a running back, he was already 28 years old. He knew that if he were to have a long career he must take advantage of every physical aid. He knew that he had especially to build up his speed.

Three months before he was due to report to the 1961 training camp, he started a special condition-

69

In the clear, Retzlaff heads for the goal.

ing program. Every day he would take time out of his hectic business life to run a few miles with lead weights on his sneakers—four pounds on each foot.

"The weight forces you to run under better control," he once explained. "You carry your natural weight better distributed. You run with better balance and better coördination. Since I've been running with weights I find that I don't get that extra jolt that used to take my eye off the ball when I have to put extra effort into running a pattern."

During a 1964 game, for example, Retzlaff, at 32, outmuscled Mel Renfro, one of the toughest, fastest young men in the league, for a pass. Then he outsprinted Renfro to the goal line.

"You old men aren't supposed to be that fast," somebody said to him after the game.

"I keep saying I'm fast—faster than ever." Retzlaff said.

Mel Renfro and the other defensive backs believe him. They wish he would retire. But Pete Retzlaff, who once wanted to quit football, has a different philosophy now.

"I enjoy this game," he says. "I really enjoy it."

5

Bill
Howton

In a dressing room deep in D.C. Stadium one day in 1963, Bill Howton was pulling on his metallic blue uniform pants. The Dallas Cowboys were about to play the Washington Redskins, and Howton was about to break the NFL career record for yardage gained by a pass receiver set by Don Hutson, the great Green Bay Packer end more than twenty years before. Howton needed only seven yards to do it. Surely he would get seven yards sometime during the afternoon. As he sat on the stool next to his locker, he was surrounded by friends and newsmen.

"When you break the record," one of them

needled him, "you ought to do something special."

"That's right," another said with a wink, "drop to one knee and sing a song. Something classy."

"Maybe I could give the ball a one-handed shot, like this," Howton said, grinning and sticking up his left hand and swinging back his right foot as if he were a ballet dancer.

Then one of the newsmen wondered what Howton would say after the game. "You ought to say," another newsman said, "'What record?' and 'Don who?'"

Howton laughed. "Don who? Imagine saying 'Don who?'"

Don Hutson and Bill Howton were good friends. Howton had started his NFL career in 1952 with the Green Bay Packers. Hutson, perhaps the NFL's most famous pass receiver, an earlier hero in Green Bay, had retired several years before. But he had settled in Racine, Wisconsin, and he was around the Packers much of the time. In recent years, as Howton neared Hutson's record, they had kidded each other about it.

"You'll never break my records," Hutson once said, smiling.

"Yes, I will," Howton replied, "and somebody will come along and break *my* records."

"That's right," Hutson agreed. "That's the game."

Now, in the moments before Howton would try to break the record, the newsmen cleared out of the locker room. Bill went over to talk to Don Meredith, who would start at quarterback for the Cowboys. The game plan called for a pass to Howton on the first play.

"The sideline pattern," Meredith said. "Let's get the record quick so you can forget about it."

The first time the Cowboys had the ball, Meredith called the play. At the snap Howton ran out a few yards and cut toward the sideline. Meredith threw and Howton caught the pass for an apparent 13-yard gain. But the Cowboys had been offside. The play was nullified. No record. Howton trotted back into the huddle.

"Sorry, Bill," said his teammate who had been offside.

"Forget it," Howton said. "We've got all day to do this."

Several plays later, the Cowboys were on the Redskin 23-yard line. Meredith moved back to pass, but he was trapped by a hard rush. Seeing Howton racing toward the end zone, Meredith put the ball into the air. Howton reached up and caught it for an apparent touchdown.

75

But a flag was down. Another penalty. Another Cowboy receiver had interfered with a Redskin defensive back.

Again Howton trotted back to the huddle without the record. But midway in the second quarter, he lined up at split end on the left side. At the snap he ran about eight yards down the sideline, faked to the outside and angled across toward the middle of the field. Meredith put the ball in his hands, and Howton caught it for a 15-yard gain and a new NFL record for yardage by a pass receiver: an even 8,000 yards, nine more than Hutson had accumulated.

"Attention, please," the voice on the public-address system announced, "Bill Howton of the Dallas Cowboys has just set . . ."

The game was stopped. One of the officials presented Howton with the ball. Bill tossed it to one of the Cowboy trainers to keep for him until after the game. Howton caught three more passes for one touchdown and a total of 82 yards, but the Cowboys lost, 21–17. In the locker room after the game the newsmen returned to congratulate him, but there were no jokes.

"I'm proud of the record," Howton said, quietly, "but we lost."

Without realizing it, perhaps, Bill Howton

76

High in the air, Howton catches a pass in a game against the Eagles.

Howton, a few steps ahead of his defenders, is
all alone with the ball.

summed up his 11-season career in those few words. It was his misfortune never to play on a championship team. Ironically, he played for two clubs, the Green Bay Packers and Cleveland Browns, which had dominated the NFL during his career. But he played for each one at the wrong time. He joined the Packers when Green Bay was considered the "Siberia" of the NFL. Then he was traded to the Browns in 1959 when the team was rebuilding following a stretch of seven Eastern Division titles. The next year he joined the Cowboys in their inaugural season. He retired after the 1963 season, before the Cowboys moved into contention.

Howton's contribution to the NFL is in the record book: 503 pass receptions for 8,459 yards and 61 touchdowns. But as he predicted, they would be broken. Entering the 1966 schedule, Raymond Berry of the Baltimore Colts had already surpassed his record for career catches and was approaching his yardage record.

Berry has had the advantage of working with one of the great quarterbacks in NFL history, Johnny Unitas. Howton has never worked with a quarterback of quite that stature, although he has always given full credit to his quarterbacks for their part in his success. He once pointed out, "I've been blessed with wonderful quarterbacks. Tobin Rote

79

at Green Bay. Eddie LeBaron, Don Meredith."
They were all good quarterbacks, but none of them
was a Johnny Unitas.

Howton seldom outran or outmuscled defensive
backs. He relied on deception. His nickname was
"The Red Fox." His red hair, sharp facial features
and cunning green eyes made him look like a fox,
and on the field he acted like one. He was sly
instead of speedy; quick instead of powerful. But
his six-foot two-inch, 180-pound frame held up in
NFL combat.

"Howton is rawbone tough; he's an old pro,"
said the Cowboy trainer, Clint Houey. "He's always
got his body under control. He knows how and
when to fall, and that's one of the most important
things for a player to learn if he's going to stay
in this league."

Billy Harris Howton learned football at a com-
paratively late age. Born on July 3, 1930, he grew
up on his father's cotton farm in Littlefield, Texas,
near Lubbock. In elementary school and in his
freshman year at Bula High School, there weren't
enough boys to organize a football team. "At Bula,"
he says, "there were about 50 boys in the whole
school." But in 1945 his family moved to a new
farm in Plainview, Texas. As a sophomore at Plain-

view High he went out for the football team and
made it as an offensive tackle.

The next year the coach, W. C. O. Harris, shifted
him to end. "You've got good speed and good
hands," the coach told him, "and besides, you'll
never make much of a tackle."

As a senior Howton, tall and skinny at six feet
two inches and 170 pounds, was named to the
All-State team. Every college in the Southwest
Conference was trying to recruit him. One day an
assistant coach at Rice University in Houston visited
him in Plainview.

"My name's Bale," the man said. "Red Bale."

"I'm sorry, sir," Howton replied, "I didn't catch
your name. Did you say Hale or Dale?"

"Bale, son, just like a bale of cotton."

Howton smiled. "I liked him right there," he
said later. "He sounded like he was from the
country like I was."

Howton enrolled at Rice. There, under Coach
Jesse Neely and assistant coach Bale, he first learned
how to use a change of pace in running a pattern.
He learned so well that he developed into an All-
America end. Despite the honors he had received
in college, he was surprised when the Packers
selected him on the second round of the annual
NFL draft. He also was uninterested. He had a

job as coach at a fashionable private school in Houston. "I wasn't even going to report," he says. "At the time I didn't know the Packers from the Forty-Niners, and I didn't care."

His wife Sandra convinced him that he should at least try out. He agreed, and as a rookie he was spectacular. He caught 53 passes to break the Packer record for one season held by Don Hutson. His 1,231 yards not only led the NFL but was the second highest total in league history. Elroy "Crazy Legs" Hirsch had set the record the year before with 1,495 yards for the Los Angeles Rams. Oddly enough, Howton gave credit to another Ram receiver, Tom Fears, for his rookie success.

One day Howton had approached head coach Gene Ronzani. "Coach," he said, "could I borrow any old films you have on the Rams?"

Ronzani asked why Howton wanted films of the Rams, and Howton replied that he wanted to study Tom Fears. He had chosen a superb pass receiver to study. In 1950 Fears set two NFL records. He caught 84 passes during the season, and he caught 18 passes in one game, against the Packers. Hour after hour, Howton watched the film of that Ram–Packer game. He would watch how Fears moved off the line of scrimmage and faked out the defensive backs. Fears did it with finesse, as Bill Howton

Howton snags a pass for the Cowboys in a game against the Pittsburgh Steelers.

would learn to do it—with a shoulder fake, a head fake, sometimes pretending to loaf, at other times speeding downfield and hooking back to make the catch.

Howton has called Tom Fears "the greatest actor of all the pass receivers I've ever seen." He considered "Crazy Legs" Hirsch the fastest pass receiver and thought that Hutson had the best hands. But Tom Fears was the best actor.

Howton's study paid off. For his play during his rookie season he was selected to the Western Division All-Star team in the Pro Bowl. There he was teamed with one of the great passers in NFL history, Norm Van Brocklin, then with the Rams. At one stage in the game, the Western All-Stars were stalled on their own 20-yard line.

"Rookie," Van Brocklin said to Howton in the huddle, "take off down that sideline and keep running. I'll get it to you."

At the snap, Howton took off. He ran and ran. He was across midfield when he looked back, but neither the ball nor Van Brocklin was anywhere to be seen. He glanced at Emlen Tunnell, the New York Giant defensive back who was covering him. Tunnell was ignoring him.

"I figured the play must be over," Howton said later, "but I kept running anyway."

As he approached the East's 30-yard line, he glanced back again, and this time the ball was arching toward him, and the crowd was shouting. Van Brocklin, with perhaps the strongest passing arm in the NFL, hit him in full stride.

"There was nobody near me," Howton recalls. "All I had to do was prance into the end zone. It was the biggest thrill I ever had in pro football."

During the years that followed, Howton continued to catch passes against better and better defensive backs. "When I first came into the NFL," he said in 1963, "pass coverage was either zone or man-to-man. But now there are eight or ten variations of each coverage. In my first few years at Green Bay, I used to tell the quarterback in the huddle that I was going to duplicate my fake of an earlier play. The defensive back's reactions were predictable. You could expect to get the same reaction from him, and you usually did. But now you never get the same reaction twice. Defensive backs have improved so much. In the old days you could sometimes beat your man by five or ten yards. But now, unless he makes a mistake, you aren't going to beat him by more than a step or two."

"The most important thing for a pass receiver," Howton continued, "is not his speed. It's agility and maneuverability. And the longer you're around, the more moves you develop. The receiver has an advantage on the man covering him because the receiver knows where he's going and the defensive back doesn't. But after a while the good defensive backs will get to know your moves if you aren't a good actor. You have to set them up, get them used to seeing you run a certain pattern, then suddenly beat them with something different."

Howton had sure hands, one of the first requirements of a great pass receiver. If he touched a pass he almost invariably caught it. "Catching the ball is something I never worried about," he said one day shortly before his retirement. "I concentrate more on my moves, the pattern, the defensive back, the mental picture of the other men around me, the down and yardage. If you ever watched yourself drop an easy pass, you know what a fool you look like. And it doesn't do any good to worry about the defensive back hitting you, because he's going to hit you whether you catch the ball or not."

Although an established NFL star, Bill Howton always worked hard in training camp. "He's like a rookie every year," one of the Cowboy assistant coaches, Ermal Allen, once said. "He goes all out to make the club. He doesn't take anything for granted. He does every exercise, every drill all the way. Maybe that's why he's such a great receiver."

86

Howton's record testifies to his amazing ability. In his home in Houston there are two footballs which have been painted white and autographed by his Cowboy teammates. They are the footballs he was presented with when he broke the all-time NFL records for yardage and receptions and capped a long career as the league's top receiver.

6

Jimmy Orr

Jimmy Orr sat in the X-ray room at Union Memorial Hospital in Baltimore. He had tumbled onto his right shoulder during the second quarter of a 1965 game with the Philadelphia Eagles. At half-time, with pain shooting through his shoulder, he had changed into his street clothes and gone to the hospital with John Spassoff, a Baltimore Colt trainer. As they waited for the X-ray report, they listened to the game coming from the radio on a shelf of the white-walled room. "The Eagles score! The Colts trail again."

The Eagles were leading, 24–20, late in the third quarter when a white-uniformed X-ray technician appeared in doorway. "You do not have a fracture, Mr. Orr," the man said. "The X rays were negative."

"Good," Orr replied. Turning to Spasoff, he said, "Let's go to the stadium. It doesn't hurt much anymore. Maybe I can play."

Several minutes later, Orr strode into the Colt locker room at Memorial Stadium. By now the Colts had regained the lead, 27–24. It was midway in the fourth quarter. The Colts stopped an Eagle drive by intercepting an Eagle pass while Orr was being helped into his uniform by trainers and equipment men. He winced every time he had to raise his right arm but soon he had his shoulder pads on. Spasoff helped pull the white jersey with the blue "28" over his head.

Out on the field, Colt coach Don Shula was pacing the sideline when one of the trainers ran up to him. "Orr's X rays were negative," he told Shula. "He's back from the hospital and you can use him. Here he comes now."

Shula turned and saw Orr coming out of the dugout not far from the Colt bench. The sellout 60,238 crowd also recognized Jimmy Orr. Their cheers and applause swept the stadium. Many of them, listening to portable radios, knew that he had left the field with a possible fractured shoulder. Now he had returned.

As Orr approached Shula, the coach waved the little flankerback into the game. Orr ran onto the field. The Colts were in a huddle. When quarterback John Unitas saw Orr, he asked, "What are you doing here?"

"I'm all right. No fracture," Orr said.

"Can you catch the ball?" Unitas asked.

"I think so," Orr said. "Try me and see."

The Colts were on their own 33-yard line. Unitas called a pass play, but he did not throw to Orr. He flipped a short pass to halfback Lenny Moore, and Moore, breaking loose, scooted to the Eagle 22. As the Colts went into their huddle, Orr said to Unitas, "They think I'm a decoy, John. I can get loose in the corner."

At the snap, Unitas went back to pass and looked downfield. Orr was running at Eagle defensive back Al Nelson. But Nelson seemed to be ignoring him. Orr got behind Nelson. Unitas lofted his pass toward the right corner of the end zone. Wincing as he reached up, Orr caught the ball. Touchdown. The crowd exploded.

Nelson, trying to recover, crashed into Orr, knocking him down. Still clutching the ball, Orr lay still for a moment. He got up slowly. Holding his right arm at his side, he trotted toward the Colt bench to another roar of applause.

The Colts kept their lead and won 34–24. Jimmy Orr had scored the clinching touchdown. In the locker room a few minutes later he was surrounded by newsmen and photographers. He was the center of attraction, perhaps for the first time in his Colt career. He had been catching touchdown passes for years in the National Football League. But he had to endure severe pain and make a dramatic return from a hospital to earn the adulation and headlines usually reserved for his more famous teammates: quarterback Unitas, halfback Moore and pass receiver Raymond Berry.

Ray Berry holds the NFL record for the most pass receptions and is one of the most famous stars in the NFL. But he is primarily a short-yardage, sideline receiver. Orr runs deeper patterns. In addition, he often comes up with the clutch touchdown catch. "I think Jimmy is one of the great money players in the game," Unitas has said. "He is our clutch player, the man who is going to make the big catch for us. There is no better deep receiver around."

Entering the 1966 NFL schedule, Orr's average of 19.6 yards per completion was the highest of any receiver with 250 or more receptions. He had caught 296 passes for 5,808 yards and 52 touchdowns. Berry, by comparison, had caught a record

Orr fumbles a pass as he is hit by a Viking
defender.

564 passes for a near-record 8,322 yards. But his 60 touchdowns were only eight more than Orr had scored in three fewer seasons.

One day in 1965 Orr sat at his locker after practice and described the difference between Berry and himself. "Raymond uses short steps along his pass route and it will naturally take him longer to cover the same amount of yardage that I'm covering," Orr said. "I run my patterns at full speed, and I try to catch the ball while running at full speed. I'll cut after a certain number of yards, whereas Raymond is more likely to cut after counting a certain number of steps. He'll then build up his speed after making the catch. He's sure something to watch. With those long fingers of his, he practically absorbs the ball.

"But for both of us, a completion often depends on the quarterback correctly reading our moves. I may have to alter my original route if I can't get the defensive back turned around. Then the quarterback will leave the time and the place of my cut up to me—and he'll have to be ready to let the ball go at precisely the right instant or we could be in trouble with an incompletion or, worse, an interception."

Throughout the 1964 season, when the Colts won the Western Division championship, none of the more than a hundred passes thrown to Orr were intercepted. It was no accident. He runs the prescribed patterns perfectly; he does not confuse the passer. When he is battling for a ball that may be intercepted, he knocks it to the ground rather than let an opponent catch it.

"When we have a pass intercepted," Orr says, "it means our offensive unit is out of the game. I'm not getting paid to sit on the sidelines."

One of Orr's finest games occurred in 1965 against the Detroit Lions in Baltimore. He caught nine passes, more than he had ever caught in one game. Unitas had hit him with touchdown passes for 17 and 32 yards in the first quarter, and the Colts were on their way to a 31–7 victory. But Orr's best catch came in the third quarter. In the huddle Orr suggested that Unitas call the Down-and-Out pattern in which Orr runs straight downfield, then slants out toward the sidelines. Unitas agreed.

At the snap Orr ran at Lion defensive back Jimmy Hill. But Hill, an old pro, was not fooled by Orr's maneuvers. As Orr streaked down the sideline, Hill was running with him, stride for stride. Unitas threw the pass high and arching, out ahead of Orr. But this made it difficult for Orr to see it coming. Twisting his head while dashing at full speed, Orr watched the ball float down. Stretching every muscle, he reached out and snatched it from the air.

"It was the greatest catch I ever saw in my playing and coaching career," said Colt coach Don Shula later.

Orr gave the credit to Unitas. "John had to throw over my head to keep it away from Hill," he told the newsmen in the locker room. "It was a perfect pass."

"But," one of them asked, "did you really expect to catch it?"

"I *always* expect that I'm going to catch the pass," Orr said.

Most of Orr's touchdown catches in Baltimore have occurred in what has become known as Orrsville: the southeast corner of the end zone at the enclosed end of Memorial Stadium. This part of the field is near home plate on the baseball diamond and, as in most baseball fields, the ground there runs slightly downhill toward the stands to help the drainage of the field when it rains.

"Maybe I catch so many balls there," Orr says with a smile, "because I can run faster downhill. But actually, where it falls off, you can't see more than 20 or 25 yards upfield."

There is one hazard in Orrsville: the third-base dugout. To protect football players from toppling

Orr watches game films with his passing partner
Johnny Unitas.

into the dugout, sheets of plywood cover the gap. Once Orr caught a touchdown pass while running at full speed through the end zone and toward the dugout. While the sellout crowd held its breath, he used the plywood as a ramp and shot up it to the dugout roof. He is not always so lucky. Once in a game in Chicago, he crashed into a brick wall several yards behind the end zone. He bounced off it like a rubber ball.

Orr was born on October 4, 1935, in Seneca, South Carolina, then a town of less than 5,000 population in the western part of the state. His father was a doctor, and Jimmy kept him busy. As a Seneca High School star, he suffered a fractured left collarbone one season and a fractured right collarbone the next season. At the time, he was not considering pro football, or even college football. He had several athletic scholarship offers from southern colleges, but he turned down all of them. "I'm going to be a lawyer," he told one college recruiter. "I want to pay my own way so I can stick to the books."

Enrolling at the University of Georgia, he changed his mind. He went out for the freshman team. But after a few weeks, he thought that the coaches were ignoring him. One day he sought out Wally Butts, the head varsity coach. "Coach," he said, "I've enjoyed being on the freshman team, but I think I'll go back to the books. I'm not good enough to play varsity."

Butts convinced Jimmy that he figured in future varsity plans and talked him out of quitting. The next season he was on the varsity. As a senior in 1957 he led the Southeastern Conference in pass receptions. Several NFL teams sent him routine questionnaires. Suddenly he wanted to play pro football. But he had his doubts. He was only 5 feet 11 inches tall and weighed only 170 pounds. "The pros are awful big, Jimmy," one of the Georgia assistant coaches warned him. "Don't set your heart on making it."

Orr had no trouble making the South team in the annual Blue–Gray Game at Montgomery, Alabama. One of the coaches there was Sammy Baugh, the former quarterback hero of the Washington Redskins. One day after practice Orr visited Baugh's office and asked the old pro if he thought a man as small as Orr could make it in the NFL.

"You'll make it," Baugh said. "Never mind what other people say. You'll make it."

Jimmy was encouraged, but none of the NFL teams shared Baugh's confidence. More than 250 college players were selected in the annual draft before the Los Angeles Rams picked him in the twenty-second round. He was their final selection. At training camp in the summer of 1958 he survived the first few roster-cuts, but the Rams had two veteran receivers in Tom Fears and Elroy Hirsch and several other outstanding prospects, all taller and stronger than Jimmy Orr. In the first three preseason games, Orr did not play. But in the fourth exhibition game, against the Pittsburgh Steelers, Ram coach Sid Gillman put him in for the final minutes. Moments later, Orr shot down the sideline and caught a pass for an 87-yard touchdown play.

But Gillman was not impressed. He still believed that Jimmy Orr was "too small" for the NFL. Several days later, the Rams were negotiating a trade with the Steelers. The Rams wanted to trade Billy Ray Smith, a defensive tackle, and the Steelers offered a future draft choice for Smith. But before closing the deal, Buddy Parker, the Steeler coach, remembered the little receiver who had caught the pass for the 87-yard touchdown play. He asked that Orr be included in the deal. Gillman doubted that the Steelers would use him much either, so he agreed.

Instead of being cut, Jimmy Orr moved in as a regular receiver in the Steeler offensive unit. Bobby

Layne, who had passed the Detroit Lions to two
NFL championships, was the Steeler quarterback.
Layne was a tough-talking quarterback in a huddle.
Shortly after Orr joined the Steelers, Layne called
a play in which Orr was the primary receiver. Then
he growled, "If you drop the pass, don't bother to
come back to the huddle."

Orr did not drop the pass. Soon he became one
of Layne's favorite receivers. In a game with the
Philadelphia Eagles, Orr was running a sideline
pattern and, as he caught Layne's pass, he was
squashed by two Eagle tacklers. He went down in
a heap, groggy from the impact, and as he lay
stretched out on the field, Layne ran up to him.

"Are you okay, Jimmy?" Layne asked.

"Did I hold the ball?" Orr replied.

"Yes, you got a first down," Layne replied. "But
get off the field. You're half knocked out."

"All right," Orr said, "but I'll be back after one
play."

He *was* back after one play. He went on to
catch 33 passes that season for 910 yards and seven
touchdowns. He was voted the NFL Rookie of the
Year in the Associated Press poll of sportswriters.
He received almost twice as many votes as the
runner-up, Bobby Mitchell, then with the Cleveland
Browns.

As Orr goes up for the pass, a Lion defensive man
brings him down again.

In 1961 Orr was traded again. This time he went to the Colts in a deal for defensive tackle Gene "Big Daddy" Lipscomb and center Buzz Nutter. He got off to a poor start in Baltimore. Bothered by pulled leg muscles, he caught only 18 passes in 1961. But in 1962 he caught 55, setting a personal record for one season. He added 41 receptions in 1963, 40 in 1964 and 45 in 1965. He also was selected as the flankerback on the 1965 All-NFL team named by the Associated Press.

Orr has proved that even in professional football there is a place for the little man—if he can catch passes and score touchdowns like Jimmy Orr.

7

Del Shofner

The New York Giants were filing out of their locker room on the way to a midweek practice in Yankee Stadium. Near the door Del Shofner sat in front of his locker. He was studying his playbook, but he was not dressed for the workout.

"You'll be late," a teammate said to him.

"I can't work out," Shofner said to him. "Bad leg."

"What's wrong?"

"I've got a pulled muscle."

His teammate laughed.

"Guess what?" he yelled to the other players. "Slim has a pulled muscle."

The others laughed, too.

"I didn't know Slim had any muscles," one of them said.

Shofner has several nicknames: Slim, The Thin Man, The Two-Iron. At six feet three inches and 185 pounds, he is among the thinnest players in National Football League history. But he also is among the swiftest and the most surehanded. When the Giants swept to Eastern Division championships in 1961, 1962 and 1963, Del Shofner caught more passes (185) for more yards (3,449) and more touchdowns (32) than any other NFL receiver. In addition, he became the only NFL receiver ever to gain more than 1,000 yards in four different seasons. He had accomplished it once with the Los Angeles Rams and three times with the Giants. His frail frame and assorted ailments made his statistics all the more spectacular.

In his own way, however, Del Shofner was as tough as most of the bigger, rougher players in the NFL. In a 1962 game, for example, as he caught a pass and turned upfield, two Pittsburgh Steeler tacklers smashed him to the ground. He fell heavily on his left shoulder and pain seared through it. Moments later, he sat on the edge of a rubbing table in the trainer's room. Dr. Francis Sweeny, the Giant team physician, was cutting away Shofner's blue jersey with a pair of scissors.

106

Several minutes later, he was on his way to a hospital. X rays showed what appeared to be a fracture of the shoulder. Dr. Sweeny told Giant coach Allie Sherman that Shofner would be out six weeks or more.

The next morning, when Shofner awoke in his hospital bed, he yawned and unconsciously stretched his arms. Moments later, he realized that there was no pain in his shoulder. He buzzed for a nurse.

"Call Doctor Sweeny," he told her, "and tell him I'd like to see him right away."

Several years earlier Shofner had broken his shoulder. When Dr. Sweeny re-examined the X rays, he noticed that the old injury had photographed as if it had been a new fracture. Shofner's shoulder was not broken, it was merely dislocated.

On Wednesday Shofner reported for practice. His left arm was strapped to his side. He couldn't catch any passes, but he was able to jog around. He knew he had to keep his legs in shape. His amazing legs were the advantage he had over other pass receivers.

The Giants were preparing for an important game with the Detroit Lions. All week Coach Sherman kept saying that Shofner might play in 10 days. On Sunday, however, Shofner went into

107

Sherman's office before the game. The shoulder feels pretty good, Coach," Shofner said in his Texas twang. "If you need me for a couple of plays, I'm ready."

Sherman couldn't believe it. After talking to Dr. Sweeny, he devised a plan: he would use Shofner as a decoy. Without the ball, Shofner wouldn't be likely to be tackled, lessening the risk of re-injury. But Sherman knew he would have to save Shofner for a crucial situation.

It developed in the second half. The Giants had moved across midfield. When Shofner lined up and raced down the sideline at the snap, two Lion defensive backs went with him. The Giant fullback, Alex Webster, cut over the middle into the territory vacated by one of the Lions covering Shofner. Y. A. Tittle, the Giant quarterback, hit Webster with a pass, and Webster bulled to the 10-yard line. Moments later Don Chandler kicked the field goal which proved to be the winning points in a 17–14 battle. When the game was over, newsmen surrounded Dr. Sweeny. They wanted an explanation of how Shofner was able to play.

"That was a trick play," the team physician pointed out. "Del isn't ready for real contact yet. He won't be able to play next week, but maybe two weeks from now."

A week after his shoulder injury, Shofner grabs
a pass from Y.A. Tittle in a game against the
Redskins.

The next week, Shofner fooled Dr. Sweeny again. He not only played, he caught 11 passes and set a Giant record with 260 yards in a 49–34 victory over the Washington Redskins. The triumph kept the Giants moving toward another Eastern Division title.

Born on December 11, 1934, in Center, Texas, Del grew up in a family of five sisters and one brother. His father was a carpenter. At Center High School he earned 11 varsity letters for football, basketball, baseball and track and field—despite an anemia condition. But the illness did not discourage the college recruiters. He was offered an athletic scholarship to Baylor University in Waco, Texas.

"I'm too light to play college football," he told the Baylor scout. "I'm only 160 pounds. But I can play basketball."

"Do me a favor," the Baylor man said. "Go out for the freshman football team before you make up your mind."

Shofner agreed. But he soon was shunted to the third team. He was playing left halfback. One day two of the right halfbacks were bothered with injuries. "Shofner," one of the coaches barked. "Let's see you run some plays from right halfback."

He impressed the coaches in practice. He impressed them even more in games. On one of his first plays, he returned a kickoff 98 yards for a touchdown. The next year, he was a varsity starter. In his junior year, the anemia and a serious case of stomach ulcers sapped his strength. But as a senior in 1956 he sparked Baylor to a Sugar Bowl upset of Tennessee. He led the team in seven categories that season: rushing, pass receiving, scoring, punt returns, kickoff returns, pass interceptions and punting. His 60 points and 40.7-yard punting average also led the Southwest Conference. He also ran the anchor leg on a 440-yard relay team which tied the world record of 40.2 seconds.

Surprisingly, he had avoided serious injury. One reason for this was the knowledge he had gained as a sprinter. "I learned in track," Shofner has said, "that you can get a lot more speed out of your body if you keep it loose. If you tighten it up, you're bound to lose speed. In football, it's important to keep loose for another reason: it absorbs the contact better."

The NFL teams were impressed with his speed. But they also were impressed with his durability. He was high on each club's list for the annual draft of college players. That winter the Los Angeles Rams had two first-round choices: their own and the rights to the New York Giants' first choice.

Shofner shows his speed on an end run for Baylor.

They had received the Giants' choice in an earlier trade.

The Rams selected halfback Jon Arnett of Southern California as their own first choice. With the New York selection, they picked Del Shofner of Baylor.

As a rookie in 1957, Shofner was used as a defensive back. The next season Ram coach Sid Gillman put him at split end. He led the league with 57 receptions and gained 1,097 yards. At the end of the season, he was named to the All-NFL team. In 1959 he had another big season: 47 receptions, 936 yards and more All-NFL honors.

But one morning in 1960 he woke up gasping for breath. There was blood in his mouth. His ulcers had returned. That season he hardly played. He caught only 12 passes for 122 yards. While he suffered, two other receivers, Jim "Red" Phillips and Carroll Dale, impressed the Ram coaches.

When the team reported to training camp in 1961, coach Bob Waterfield had his mind made up that Phillips and Dale would be his two wide receivers. Del Shofner would be their substitute. Then at training camp a rookie, Duane Allen, looked good enough to move in ahead of Shofner.

At dinner one evening Waterfield was chatting with Elroy Hirsch, the Ram general manager.

113

"Maybe we can make a trade for Shofner," the coach said. "We could get something for him." Hirsch agreed, suggesting that they trade for the Giants' first choice in the college draft. He had his eye on Roman Gabriel, a quarterback at North Carolina State. Hirsch dispatched one of his aides to find out if the Giants were interested.

The Ram aide mentioned that Shofner might be available to a Giant official. The Giant man shrugged. He didn't want to let the Forty-Niners know that the Giants really wanted Shofner. As soon as the conversation ended, however, the Giant official reported to Wellington Mara, one of the Giant owners and perhaps the shrewdest trader in the NFL. Mara called Hirsch, who confirmed that Shofner was available.

"What's wrong with him?" Mara asked, suspiciously. "He was the best receiver in the league a couple of years ago."

"I don't think anything's really wrong with him," Hirsch said, "but the coaches have lost confidence in him."

Mara asked for time. He wanted to find out what his Giant veterans thought of Shofner. He went first to Dick Lynch, the veteran cornerback who had covered Shofner in previous seasons, and asked, "How did Shofner look to you?"

114

Shofner reaches for the ball as the defender makes
one last lunge.

"He's as tough a pass receiver as I ever covered," Lynch replied. "He looked as good last time we played as he ever did."

Mara then went to Y. A. Tittle, the veteran quarterback obtained a few weeks earlier from the San Francisco Forty-Niners. "I played with Del in the Pro Bowl a few years ago," Tittle said, "and he was the best receiver I ever threw to."

Finally Mara consulted with coach Allie Sherman. The draft choice, they realized, could not possibly help them until the following season. But Shofner would help right away. Mara called Hirsch again and closed the deal. The Giants didn't realize it at the time, but they got more than Del Shofner. They got three Eastern Division titles.

The day Shofner reported, however, the Giants wondered about the wisdom of the trade. The Giants were in their training camp at Fairfield, Connecticut. Shofner boarded an evening plane in Los Angeles bound for New York. He got no sleep on the flight. Arriving in New York, he took a cab to Grand Central Station and hopped on a train. But the train did not stop at Fairfield. It roared through to Bridgeport. Shofner got off there and took a taxicab back to Fairfield. He checked into the Giant camp at breakfast time. One of the first players to greet him was Tittle.

116

Del fumbles the ball while being hurried by an "invisible" defender.

"Del is not the healthiest looking guy in the world when he is at his best," Tittle once recalled. "In addition to his ulcers, he has a sallow skin. But if you could have seen him that morning, you wouldn't have believed it. His eyes were sunk back in his face, his complexion was paler than usual. He was drawn and tired looking. His hair was mussed. He reminded me of a walking scarecrow."

His appearance shocked other Giants. One of them said, "He looks like a clarinet player after a hard one-night stand."

But in the next few days his teammates' opinion changed. Shofner was flashing his old speed on the fly pattern, the one in which he flies downfield to race under a long pass. The Giants had never had a receiver with such speed. The two veteran quarterbacks, Charley Conerly and Tittle, began to depend on him. Either on a long pass or on a short sideline pass in a third-down situation, Shofner invariably was their target. That season Shofner caught 68 passes for 1,125 yards and 11 touchdowns. In 1962 he caught 53 for 1,133 yards and 12 touchdowns. In 1963 he caught 64 for 1,181 yards and nine touchdowns.

"Notice how consistent he was those three years," says Frank Gifford, a former Giant teammate of Shofner's. "Del was the best all-around receiver

Veterans Tittle and Shofner watch a Giant
practice.

I ever saw. Raymond Berry of the Colts may be able to fake better, but he isn't going to catch many short turnouts, at five or ten yards, and turn them into long touchdowns. When Del walks up to the line of scrimmage, he scares a lot of defensive backs because they know he's got such terrific speed that he can give a little head fake and get behind them."

Jesse Whittenton, a defensive cornerback for the Green Bay Packers who covered Shofner twice in NFL championship games, had a reputation for stopping him. "I didn't stop him," Whittenton once said. "I was lucky. He beat me bad a couple of times, but the pass went to the other side of the field. Del runs with a glide, where you don't know whether he's going at full speed or loafing on you. And when you find out, it's too late. He has a great sense of timing and great hands, so about the only way to stop him is to hold him. And when you do that, it's a penalty. You can't win."

During those three title seasons with the Giants, Shofner roomed with Y. A. Tittle. One day, on a road trip, Shofner was walking through a hotel lobby carrying two bags—his own and Tittle's. "What's going on?" somebody asked Del. "Do you do this so Y. A. will throw to you?"

"No," Del answered with a wink. "I've made a deal with Y. A. I carry his bag, and he promises not to call any of the plays where I'm supposed to have a blocking assignment."

Del Shofner didn't have to worry. Y. A. Tittle's philosophy was "to put the ball in the air," and he wanted Del Shofner out there where he could catch it.

8

Dante Lavelli and Mac Speedie

One day shortly after the Cleveland Browns won the 1964 National Football League championship, the club publicity man, Nate Wallack, was working at his desk in the team offices in huge Municipal Stadium near Lake Erie. He was revising the individual records in the club's history. When he came to the section on pass receiving, he glanced up at a visitor.

"Look at this," Wallack said. "I don't have to make any changes here."

His visitor checked the records. Of the 10 record categories, Gary Collins, the flanker on the 1964 championship team, held one record, set in 1963.

123

The other nine were shared by two pass catchers out of the past, Dante Lavelli and Mac Speedie. Lavelli had five, Speedie four.

"They formed maybe the best pair of pass catchers in pro football history," Wallack said. "Some receivers may have been better than either one, but I don't think any team ever had as brilliant a pair of pass catchers."

When Mac Speedie was a youngster, it appeared he would never even walk properly, much less develop into a football star. Born on January 12, 1920, in Odell, Illinois, he was christened Mac by his Scottish grandfather. In later years his name confused some people. They assumed it was a nickname for Macgregor or Macdougall. Other people thought his name was Max. Paul Brown often introduced him as Max MacSpeedie. As a boy, however, his name was the least of his problems. He developed a bone deficiency in his left leg. By the time he was eight years old, he was a cripple. His left leg was two inches shorter than his right.

Doctors told Mac that the only way to correct the condition was to fit a steel brace that would gradually stretch the underdeveloped leg. He would have to wear the brace for at least two or

124

three years. Although he didn't like the idea of being held down by the brace for so long, Speedie finally agreed to submit to the treatment when doctors assured him that one day he would be able to run and to go out for sports again.

The brace extended from his hip to his ankle. Every week the doctor would adjust a screw on the brace which lengthened it, gradually stretching the leg. The weeks dragged into months and into years. All the time Mac Speedie was dreaming of the day when he would be able to play football and basketball and baseball as his companions did. One day, when Mac was 12, four years after the brace had been fitted, the doctor took it off and inspected Mac's left leg.

"Your leg is fine," the doctor said. "It's the same length as your other leg." Handing the brace to Mac, he said, "Throw this thing away. You don't need it any more."

All the athletic ambition that Speedie had stored up now burst forth. He began to play football and basketball and to run on the track team. "I don't suppose that I would ever have been ambitious enough to excel at any sport if I hadn't been a cripple as a kid," he said later. "I spent so much time eating my heart out because I couldn't play normally that when they took the brace off and I

125

found I had legs that matched, it was like turning a frisky colt out to pasture after a year in a box stall. Kids who are healthy sometimes don't appreciate what a blessing it is."

By the time Mac reached high school, his family had moved to Salt Lake City, Utah. He became an All-City halfback and an All-City basketball center at Salt Lake's South High School. He then enrolled at the University of Utah, where he was moved to end and was picked for the All-Rocky Mountain Conference team. His best sport in college, however, was track. He once ran the 100-yard dash in 9.8 seconds. In the 220-yard low hurdles, he set a conference record with a time of 23.2. He shared the conference record for the 120-yard high hurdles with a 14.4 clocking. His fastest time in the high hurdles was never clocked, however. In one meet, he pushed Fred Wolcott of Rice Institute to a world record time of 13.7. Speedie was a close but unclocked second.

Mac majored in geology at Utah hoping to become an oil research specialist. But when he was graduated from college, the United States was fighting World War II, and he entered the Army instead. One day when he was stationed in Texas, Fred Mandel, then the owner of the Detroit Lions,

126

visited him. Mandel was hoping to sign Speedie to a contract for the first year after the war.

Mandel showed him a contract calling for $2,800 a season. "You'll be the second-highest-paid lineman in the NFL," Mandel said.

Mac was ready to sign. He asked Mandel for a pen, but Mandel kept talking. Speedie again asked for a pen. But Mandel still ignored the request. "After a while," Speedie disclosed later, "I was practically begging him for the pen, but he must have changed his mind. He told me we might as well wait until the war was over. He put the contract in his pocket, and I never heard from him again."

He heard from other teams, however. While stationed at Fort Warren, in Wyoming, he received a bid from the owners organizing the Chicago Rockets in the new All-America Conference. As quarterback of the base team, he had a chance to see the future Rocket players in action when he played against the El Toro Marine Base team. Several of the El Toro players had already been signed by the Rockets. "The way they swarmed in on me," Speedie said, "I was sure they would be a terrific pro team."

Fortunately, Speedie received an even better offer

Mac Speedie goes high in the air to catch a pass from Otto Graham.

from the Cleveland Browns in the All-America Conference before he signed with the Rockets. The Rockets were the poorest team in the new conference, losing all but eight of their first 45 games and finally going broke.

The Cleveland offer came from Paul Brown, for whom the new team was to be named. Brown had been the coach of the powerful Massillon (Ohio) High School teams and of Ohio State University before the war. During the war, he had done an outstanding job as football coach at the Great Lakes Naval Base near Chicago. He had seen Speedie play for the Fort Warren base team and offered him a place with the Browns. Speedie signed. When the Browns opened the 1946 AAC season, Mac scored the first touchdown in the league's history.

Lavelli was born three years after Speedie on February 13, 1923, and grew up in Hudson, Ohio, then a town of less than 2,000 residents southeast of Cleveland. At Hudson High School he was a three-sport star: a quarterback in football, a high-scoring forward in basketball and a hard-hitting first baseman in baseball. The Detroit Tigers offered him a baseball contract, but Dante turned it down to go to college.

Lavelli entered Ohio State on a football scholar-

129

ship. Working out at halfback on the freshman team, he was running through a play one day when Paul Brown, then the varsity coach, noticed the way he seemed to glide across the ground. Brown preferred his halfbacks to use short, choppy steps to make it easier for them to cut. "The Lavelli boy runs more like an end," Brown told one of the freshman coaches. "Let's try him there."

As a sophomore, Lavelli was a varsity end. But after a few appearances, he was sidelined by an injury. The next year he was in the army. As a sergeant leading a rifle platoon, he served in combat in France, Belgium and Germany, including the famous Battle of the Bulge. "We had no time for football," he once said, "but every so often we'd fool around, using a canteen for a ball."

After Lavelli's discharge at the end of the war, Paul Brown offered him a 1946 contract with the Browns. Dante protested that he wasn't ready for the pros. He had hardly played varsity football at Ohio State, and he wanted to go back to get his education. Brown assured him that he'd make the team and that he could attend college in the off-season.

Lavelli finally agreed. But when he reported to training camp he was still skeptical about his chances of making the team. There were four other

130

candidates for the right end position. One was an experienced pro player, and two others had played for powerful service teams during the war. The other candidate was an All-America player from Notre Dame, John Yonaker.

One by one, the other players were released. Soon only Lavelli and Yonaker remained. Then one day at practice Lavelli noticed Yonaker drilling with the defensive unit. Brown had decided to convert him into a defensive end. Lavelli was the regular offensive right end. His inexperience increased his eagerness to learn everything he could. He soon discovered that pro football was much different from the game played in college and high school.

"In college," he said, "when you come out of a game, you sit on the bench and relax. But not in the pros."

In one of his first games with the Browns, Lavelli trotted off the field after an unsuccessful series of downs. One of the Brown bench warmers walked over to him and said, "The defensive back is giving you the inside. You can beat him there with a good fake."

Lavelli looked up, surprised. He used the suggestion, and it worked for a first down. "That's what I mean about the pros," he said. "Everybody

131

Otto Graham (left) and Dante Lavelli show off in
the clubhouse after winning the 1946 All-America
Conference title.

on the bench is awake. Everybody is a real student. The coaches even more so. Football is a real challenge with the Browns."

With Lavelli and Speedie at the ends, Otto Graham at quarterback and Paul Brown on the sidelines, the Browns completely dominated the new All-America Conference. They won the championship every year for four seasons with little competition. They were so good that they ruined the league. In 1950 the AAC suspended operation, and the NFL absorbed three teams—the Browns, the Baltimore Colts and the San Francisco Forty-Niners. Speedie and Lavelli had been selected to most of the All-AAC All-Star teams in those four years and had set several league records. Now they had to prove they were equal to NFL competition.

They proved it in their first NFL game against the 1949 champion Philadelphia Eagles. Speedie caught a 13-yard touchdown pass, Lavelli a 26-yard touchdown pass. Otto Graham completed 21 of 38 passes for 346 yards and three touchdowns, and the Browns routed the Eagles 35–10. The Browns were already on their way to dominating the NFL as they had the AAC. They won the Eastern Division title and in the NFL championship game, Lavelli caught two touchdown passes in a 30–28 triumph over the Los Angeles Rams.

133

During the seven seasons Lavelli and Speedie played together on the Browns, the team won seven divisional titles and five league championships. Lavelli went on to play four more seasons, during which the Browns added three more divisional crowns and two NFL championships. In those years, the Brown quarterback was the great Otto Graham, now coach of the Washington Redskins. Some people claim that Graham's talent made it easy for Lavelli and Speedie. But Graham disagrees. "They made it easy for *me*," he says. "All I had to do was throw the ball into the air and one of those guys would go and get it."

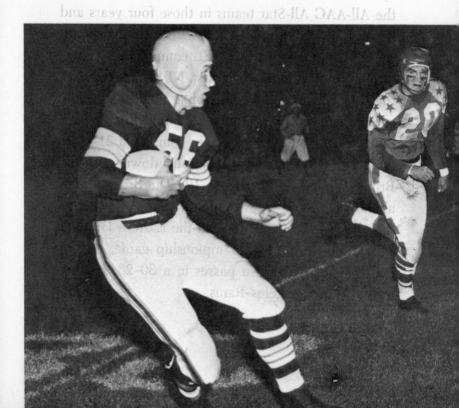

Lavelli and Speedie collaborated for some startling statistics during their Brown careers. Lavelli caught 396 passes for 6,478 yards and 62 touchdowns, all records for a member of the Browns. Speedie caught 349 for 5,572 yards and 33 touchdowns. Entering the 1966 NFL schedule, Speedie still held two Browns season records: 67 catches and 1,146 yards, both set in 1947. He also held the single-game records for most receptions, 11, and most yards, 228. Lavelli's two other club records were his four touchdown catches in one game and his streak of catching at least one pass in 31 consecutive games.

Lavelli takes a pass and heads for the goal.

Speedie takes a Graham pass as Cleveland defeats the 1951 College All-Stars.

As similar as were their successes, their styles and personalities were different. Lavelli was studious, Speedie carefree. "But each is supreme in his own way," their coach, Paul Brown, once said. "I think Lavelli has the strongest hands I've ever seen. When he goes up for a pass and a defensive back goes up with him, you can be sure Dante will have the ball when they come down. Nobody can ever take it away from him once he gets his hands on it. Speedie is perhaps a more instinctive pass receiver, and a little more deceptive. He's so tall that when he's running at top speed, he seems to be gliding easily. His natural ability to change pace and his great speed when he turns it on makes it almost impossible to cover him with less than three men. I believe Lavelli does more conscious thinking about his movements than Mac does. Lavelli plans his faking, whereas Speedie seems to do his instinctively. They've got two things in common— they can catch anything you can throw, and after they've caught it, they both run like halfbacks."

In action, Lavelli was outspokenly confident, while Speedie waited patiently for the proper pass pattern to develop. On almost every play, Lavelli would come into the huddle and tell Graham, "I'm open. Throw it to me." And no matter what play was used, Lavelli would be shouting, "Otto, Otto" as he ran his pattern. Speedie, by comparison,

137

seldom said a word to Graham. He preferred to set up the defensive back covering him for a certain pattern. When he did, he would tell Graham in the huddle or Coach Brown on the sidelines. "The sideline is open now," Speedie might say. "Any time you want to use it." When Speedie said so, he was almost always clear, and quite often the play would work for a touchdown.

Lavelli completed his education at Ohio State during the off-seasons, receiving his degree in 1949. When he retired after the 1956 season he became a businessman in Cleveland.

Mac Speedie preferred to stay in football. He joined the Houston Oilers of the American Football League in 1960 as an assistant coach. In 1962 he moved to the Denver Broncos to take charge of their pass receivers. Two years later he took over in midseason as head coach of the Broncos.

As a coach, Speedie became a popular after-dinner speaker. One of his favorite stories involves Dante Lavelli. He tells how the Browns used to needle Lavelli for thinking he was always open and for shouting, "Otto, Otto" to get the attention of quarterback Otto Graham. It got to be such a habit that, in 1956, Lavelli's final season, he occasionally would run his pattern and turn for the ball and yell, "Otto, Otto."

138

"The only thing is," Speedie says with a laugh, "Otto had retired the previous year. George Ratterman was the quarterback."

9

Dave
Parks

High above the clouds, the San Francisco Forty-
Niners relaxed in their chartered airliner. Several
hours earlier on this October day in 1965, they had
lost to the Baltimore Colts 27–24. But despite the
defeat, the Forty-Niner players and coaches were
not discouraged. They had played well—especially
Dave Parks, who had caught three touchdown
passes, tying a club record. He had also set a
Forty-Niner record by gaining 231 yards.

Several seats away sat three Forty-Niner heroes
of past years: quarterback Y. A. Tittle and two of
his favorite pass receivers, Billy Wilson and Gordy
Soltau. Tittle and Wilson had returned to the

Forty-Niners as assistant coaches. Soltau was a TV announcer. Soltau had held the Forty-Niner record of yards gained on pass receptions that Parks had broken.

Tittle, Wilson and Soltau were chatting with some San Francisco sportswriters. "Parks is a great one," Soltau said. "This is only his second year in the league and he's great already."

"The way he's going," Tittle said, "he'll be on the All-NFL team. He's something."

"But it wasn't just his catches," Wilson pointed out. "It was the way he was fighting for the ball and moving after he caught it. I can't put any limit on his future. It isn't his beating the defensive backs and catching the ball that makes him outstanding. It's what he does after he gets it. He has a tremendous desire to score. If it's humanly possible, he'll score. It takes a solid tackle to get him. He could have been a great running back. Another thing about him, he's the best blocking wide end in the league. He's great at it. He's just a great all-around athlete."

In two seasons in the National Football League, six-foot-two, 207-pound Dave Parks had established himself as a threat to break all records for pass receivers. He led the league in 1965 with 80 receptions and 1,344 yards. His two-year totals were 116 receptions for 2,047 yards and 20 touch-downs. Entering the 1966 schedule, he already held four Forty-Niner records and shared another.

His 80 receptions in 1965 shattered the old Forty-Niner record of 60, set by Billy Wilson. His 1,344 yards gained surpassed the old record of 1,032. In his rookie year he set another club mark by gaining an average of 19.5 yards per reception. His fourth record, of course, was his 236-yard performance against the Colts. His three touchdowns that day tied a fifth record.

Adding to the drama of his performance that day in Baltimore was the situation. The Colts had jumped into a 17–0 lead in the second quarter. On the sideline Forty-Niner coach Jack Christiansen told quarterback John Brodie, "Throw the ball. We've got to get some points on the board."

Whenever Brodie threw, Dave Parks was there to catch the ball. On the first touchdown play, the Forty-Niners were on their own 47-yard line. Parks moved across the line of scrimmage, faked Colt defensive back Lenny Lyles and streaked for the end zone. Brodie hit him for a 53-yard touchdown play.

The Colts then scored another touchdown to go ahead, 24–7, at the half. In the third quarter, the Forty-Niners were on the Colt 45 when Brodie spun

143

and pitched out to halfback John David Crow. Again Parks loped downfield as Crow moved out around left end on the run-pass option play. Crow saw Parks break loose and threw him a pass for a 45-yard touchdown.

Early in the fourth quarter, the Forty-Niners again moved into Colt territory. In the third-and-ten situation on the Colt 15, Brodie moved back behind his pass blockers and looked for a receiver. Parks was alone in the end zone. Brodie fired his pass. The Forty-Niner tight end, Monty Stickles, not realizing Parks was open behind him, stuck up one of his hands in a desperate effort to catch the ball. Stickles couldn't hold onto it, and he deflected it away from Parks. Incomplete. The Forty-Niners had to settle for a field goal and trailed, 24–17.

The Colts added another field goal for a 27–17 lead, but Parks kept the Forty-Niners in the game. With the ball on the Colt 46, Brodie called another pass play in which Parks was the primary receiver. This time Parks had to outleap and outmuscle Colt defensive back Alvin Haymond for the ball. When they came down, Haymond nearly tackled Parks, but the big Forty-Niner shook him off and pranced into the end zone. Another touchdown.

But that was all the Forty-Niners could do. The Colts held on for a 27–24 victory. "That Parks is

144

Parks holds the ball tight as Detroit defensive
back Dick LeBeau gets set to pull him down.

a real receiver," Don Shula, the Colt coach, said in his dressing room. "He's as good a receiver as we've had in the league in a long time."

Dave Parks entered the NFL as a surprise selection. During his senior season at Texas Tech, Parks was named to several All-America teams. But as the NFL clubs gathered in Chicago in 1963 for the annual draft of college talent, it appeared that several other players would be picked ahead of him. The Forty-Niners would receive first choice of all the eligible college players, and it was rumored that they would pick George Mira, the quarterback from Miami University. There were other prospects as well: running backs, quarterbacks, pass receivers and linemen.

Two days before the NFL draft, Parks had been an inconspicuous fourth-round-choice draft of the American Football League. Parks himself assumed that the Dallas Cowboys would be the NFL team which would draft him. The day before the NFL draft he had been a guest of the Cowboys at a game with the New York Giants. But that same day Lou Spadia, the Forty-Niner general manager, arrived to talk with Parks.

"We want to draft you number one," Spadia told him. Parks was surprised and flattered. "But we don't want to waste our choice," Spadia continued. "You've got to agree to sign with us."

Parks refused to guarantee that he would sign with the Forty-Niners, because he had not received a formal offer from the San Diego Chargers, who had picked him in the AFL draft. Spadia described the Forty-Niner offer, but would not promise to top the best San Diego offer. Parks refused to promise anything until he had seen the Chargers' offer.

Spadia was perplexed. He called the Forty-Niner president, Vic Morabito, in San Francisco. "I don't know what to tell you," Spadia told him. "Parks won't promise to sign if we draft him."

Morabito wanted to consider the problem overnight and call Spadia back before the draft started in the morning. He had to be up early. The draft meeting in Chicago started at 7:00 A.M., San Francisco time. Before seven, Morabito phoned Spadia in Texas. "Has Parks changed his mind?" he asked.

"Not yet," Spadia reported. "He wants to think about the Charger offer no matter what we do."

"He's too good to lose," Morabito said. "Let's pick him and take our chances on signing him."

Morabito then dialed one of the Forty-Niner phones at the draft meeting in Chicago. "We're picking Dave Parks of Texas Tech," he told his assistants. Moments later, at the rostrum at one

147

end of the room, NFL Commissioner Pete Rozelle adjusted the microphone and announced, "The San Francisco Forty-Niners select Dave Parks, an end, from Texas Tech."

The room buzzed with surprise. Dave Parks was surprised, too. Later that day he told a newsman, "I'm still in shock about being the number one choice in the whole league. But as for signing, I'm going to play for the team that gives me the best deal."

The Forty-Niners apparently offered the best deal. Four days later, Parks signed. Spadia went back to San Francisco much relieved. "I spent about five days with Parks," he said at the time, "but I didn't dare take a deep breath until I got his name on the contract."

David Wayne Parks was born on Christmas Day, 1941, in St. Jo, Texas, a tiny town of less than 1,000 residents near the Oklahoma border. His father worked on an oil-drilling rig. When young Dave was about to enter the sixth grade, his father found a better job in Abilene, Texas. Transferring to Bowie Elementary School, Dave began to play organized football for the first time. He enjoyed playing half-back, but he was too small.

One day the following year at Lincoln Junior

High School, he was playing catch with a small rubber football in the dirt schoolyard. He accidentally stepped into a hole and broke several small bones in his right foot. The injury ended his seventh-grade football season.

The next year when he reported for practice, Dave tried out at halfback. But the team had several hard-running halfbacks, all of them huskier than he was. One day the coach called him aside and said, "Dave, I'm going to move you to right end. You'll have a better chance there."

Parks was soon a regular. For the next two years he played on the Abilene High School junior varsity. As a junior he not only made the varsity squad, he made the All-District team. As a senior he was selected for the All-State team. He was offered several scholarships but of all the men attempting to recruit him, he was most impressed with J. T. King, then an assistant coach at Texas Tech.

King assured Dave that he'd fit right into the Texas Tech strategy. Tech was known for its passing teams and used a pro-type offense. Dave's hero in earlier years had been pass receiver Harlon Hill of the Chicago Bears. In his daydreams, Parks saw himself running pro-type patterns the way Hill did. He decided to enroll at Texas Tech. During his

149

Parks (81) bobbles pass as Packer Dick Whittenton
bears down on him.

sophomore season, J. T. King took over as head coach. But while he attempted a pro-type offense, King did not yet have enough good players to make it work.

Over Parks's three varsity seasons, the team lost twenty games and won only ten. But Parks set several school records, catching a total of 80 passes for 1,080 yards. More important, perhaps, he was an all-around player. His coach, J. T. King, often said, "Dave Parks would be a starter on my team if he never caught a pass. He can block and tackle, and that's the name of this game." Buster Brannon, a scout for Texas Christian University, claimed, "Parks is the finest offensive end in college football."

With the Forty-Niners, Parks learned the pro game quickly. As a rookie in 1964 he led the Forty-Niners in touchdowns with eight. He caught 36 passes for 703 yards. When the season ended he was selected to play for the Western Division All-Stars in the annual Pro Bowl game in Los Angeles. He was the first Forty-Niner rookie ever named to the Pro Bowl squad.

Still, he had his embarrassing moments. With time for one more play in the first half in a game against the Chicago Bears, the Forty-Niners had the ball on the Bear 42-yard line. Coach Jack Christiansen sent in his field-goal unit. With the final

152

seconds ticking off on the clock, Parks hurried off the field. He scampered to the nearest sideline, the one in front of the Bear bench.

Kicking from the 49-yard line, Tommy Davis booted the ball high into the air. The ball floated over the crossbars and the officials raised their arms to signal it was good. But George Halas, the old coach of the Bears, was jumping up and down. "Penalty," Halas shouted at the officials. "Parks can't run off the field on our side. Penalty. Penalty."

Halas was correct. It's illegal for a player to leave the field on the opposing team's sideline. Parks had thought that since there wouldn't be time for another play, it wouldn't make any difference. But he was wrong. Parks had cost his team three vital points.

The Bears won the game 23–21. The canceled field goal had cost the Forty-Niners a victory. "The rules say that all players must leave the playing field on their team's side of the field," coach Jack Christiansen growled after the game. "The rule is the same in college as it is in the NFL. It's a rule that you expect everyone to know."

In 1965 Parks's education began to pay off. But he was still learning. Assistant coach Billy Wilson continued to teach him what to expect from opposing defensive backs and how to take advantage of

Parks takes a ballet pose as he snares a pass.

them. Day by day, he began to see things in game films that he had never really *seen* as a rookie. "My first year," he says, "I looked at those movies as much as anybody, but I wasn't *seeing* what was happening. Now I'm starting to."

Parks credits Billy Wilson with making him realize the importance of timing. "During the week we'll be looking at films together," he says, "and he'll show me how my man is overshifting to the inside in certain situations and how he'll be open to the outside. During the game, Billy sits up in the press box and he might tell me on the phone how my man is getting help from another defensive back on, say, the inside and is playing too much on the outside and that maybe a curl pattern would work against him."

Billy Wilson is teaching Dave Parks to break his Forty-Niner career record of 407 pass receptions. Parks may set NFL records as well. But he says, "I'd like to set some records; I guess every player would. But I'm not going to think about it much. I've got too many other things to think about."

Such as winning the next game and catching his next pass.

10

Bob
Hayes

Hopping out of the huddle, Bob Hayes of the Dallas Cowboys trotted toward his split-end position. Across the line of scrimmage crouched Erich Barnes, the cornerback of the Cleveland Browns.

"Well," Barnes sneered, "look who I've got, the world's fastest human."

Hayes stared back. "You better believe it," he said firmly.

By the end of the game Barnes did believe it. Hayes outran him and outfaked him and caught five passes. It was one of several spectacular 1965 games for Hayes during his rookie season in the National Football League. His accomplishments

157

were surprising to many observers. He was, indeed, the world's fastest human. In the 1964 Olympics in Tokyo he had won the Olympic 100-meter dash and anchored the victorious United States 400-meter relay team. The year before, he had set a world record with a time of 9.1 seconds in the 100-yard dash. But other star sprinters had failed to make it in the NFL.

A few sprinters have become NFL stars, notably Claude "Buddy" Young of the Baltimore Colts and Bob Boyd of the Los Angeles Rams. But in recent years three world-record runners—sprinters Frank Budd and Ray Norton and hurdler Glenn Davis— had been dropped by NFL teams. Many sprinters lack the durability and deception that are necessary in pro football. But Hayes showed once again that some track men belong on the football field. Howard "Red" Hickey, then a Cowboy assistant coach, predicted, "If nothing happens to him physically, Bob Hayes will have to be one of the all-time greats."

As a rookie Hayes caught 46 passes. Even more impressive were his 12 touchdowns and 1,003 yards. He was only the fourth rookie pass receiver in NFL history to gain more than 1,000 yards. The others were Mike Ditka of the Bears, Harlon Hill of the Bears and Bill Howton of the Green Bay

Packers. In addition, Hayes's average gain per reception of 21.8 yards led all NFL pass receivers in 1965.

Hayes's success surprised others, but it did not surprise him. "My philosophy with the Cowboys," he said, "is the same one I had when I was a sprinter. Even in qualifying races, I ran all out. Other sprinters just tried to qualify for the semifinal or the final. Not me. I tried to win every race. I figured that if somebody beats me in a race, even if it's a qualifying race, it will build his confidence. I didn't want to build anybody's confidence but my own. I wanted them to think of me as a guy who is always in there tough. I wanted them to say, 'Hayes doesn't let up.' "

Then he winked and added, "Put that on my tombstone some day: 'He never let up.' "

One of the reasons that Hayes is succeeding in pro football where other great sprinters have failed is that football has always been one of his main interests. His college football coach, Jake Gaither of Florida A. & M. says, "Bob was a football player who became an Olympic champion, not an Olympic champion who tried to be a football player. Bob came to college on a football scholarship. He just happened to be fast enough to run 9.1 in his spare time."

159

Hayes was also tough enough to enjoy the crashing contact of the NFL. He showed this during a preseason game with the Chicago Bears. The Cowboys were about to kick off when the coaches realized the kickoff unit was a man short. The player assigned to "break up the wedge," a man six feet three inches tall and weighing 225 pounds, had been injured. Breaking up the wedge means racing recklessly downfield and slamming into the first group of blockers. It is perhaps the assignment responsible for more injuries than any other in football.

"We need a man to break up the wedge," one of the Cowboy coaches shouted on the sideline.

"Let me do it," Hayes yelled, clicking the chin strap on his blue helmet. "I'll break it up."

He jogged onto the field, but before he got far Jim Meyers, the offensive line coach, ran out and grabbed him. At five feet eleven inches and only 190 pounds, Bob was hardly built for the job, and he was too valuable to risk as a wedge man. But he was ready and willing.

"That told me that Bob Hayes is a football player," Meyers says. "He sold me on himself right then."

Bob was born on December 20, 1942, in a slum

section of Jacksonville, Florida, known as Hell's Hole. He had an older brother, Ernie, who wanted to be a boxer. Even in those days Bob was confident —so confident that it annoyed his brother.

"You're too cocky," Ernie often teased.

"I am not," Bob would reply, swinging.

Then they would go at it. Bob says, "I never had the strength to knock anybody out. But he kept calling me cocky, and I kept trying."

They had friendly moments as well. To help Ernie train, Bob would do roadwork with him in the evenings. Bob ran for fun then, and it wasn't until he got to Matthew Gilbert High School that he began to take running seriously. One day in an activity period, the students had to race. Bob was matched with the school's star sprinter, and he beat him by five yards.

After watching the race, the track coach, Bill Cannon, strolled over to talk to Hayes. "I just saw you run," Cannon said. "You have natural speed. With a little coaching, you could do the 100 in 9.5. Maybe faster."

Bob agreed to go out for track. But in his first meet, on a grass track, he clocked a disappointing 10.1.

"You've been kidding me," Hayes later told the coach. "I'm no sprint runner."

"Give yourself a chance," the coach replied. "The next meet is on a cinder track."

On cinders, a faster surface, Hayes was clocked in 9.7 seconds. The next week he ran it in 9.6. He was on his way to developing into the world's fastest human. He also played football at Gilbert High, and his accomplishments earned him a football scholarship to Florida A. & M. College in Tallahassee.

During his freshman year at Florida A. & M., something occurred which would haunt Hayes for years to come. He was studying in his dormitory room when another student dropped by. Bob agreed to go downtown with him for a cup of coffee.

He should have kept studying. On the way downtown, Bob's friend drew a gun and held up a man on the street. The gun was really a water pistol, but the victim didn't know that. Neither did the Tallahassee policemen investigating the robbery. The next day the student with the "gun" was arrested and charged with robbery. He had gained six cents and two sticks of chewing gum. Bob Hayes was arrested, too, as a material witness. He was soon paroled in the custody of coach Jake Gaither and ordered to report to his probation officer once a month for ten years.

At the time, Hayes was not a famous athlete.

162

The case did not rate headlines. But in 1965, several months after his Olympic heroics and shortly before he was to report to the Cowboy training camp, the story appeared in a Miami, Florida, newspaper.

"I knew the day before that the story would be in the paper," he wrote later. "Coach Gaither was upset, and he thought I would be, too, but I had prepared myself for this long ago. I have traveled many miles for my country, my state and my school. I have given advice to many boys. Invariably, my first words are to stay out of trouble and live a clean, healthy life. When I had time to really talk to boys, I would tell them that I have been in trouble and that I was lucky to be where I am today.

"I hope that no youngster ever makes a mistake in his life," Hayes continued. "But if he does and is given another chance, I hope he tries and will do something with his life to make the people who afforded him that chance feel proud they were instrumental in his achievements."

In June, 1965, Bob was granted a full pardon by the governor of Florida, but the memory of his brush with the law remains.

As a sprinter, Hayes had an unorthodox style. Instead of gliding like a whippet, as most sprinters do, he ran with his knees unusually high, his elbows

163

Hayes slows down after winning a heat of the
100-meter dash in the Tokyo Olympics.

out wide and his toes pointed in. He even spiked himself several times. He also has an unorthodox style of training. Before the 1963 Amateur Athletic Union championships in St. Louis, he kept in shape by doing 25 sit-ups and two laps each day. The result: his 9.1 world record for 100 yards.

"You need a rest sometimes," he explained, "and the coaches don't understand this. You just have to take it easy once in a while. Overall, I train a little harder each year, and there hasn't been a year that I haven't gained speed."

Before the Tokyo Olympics, he set two other world records: 5.9 for the 60-yard dash and 6.9 for the 70-yard dash. In the Olympic 100-meter dash he was timed in 10 seconds flat, tying the world record. But his most memorable perform-ance at Tokyo occurred in the 400-meter relay. As he waited to take the baton on the anchor leg, the United States was in last place. Five other teams —France, Germany, Great Britain, Russia and Poland—were bunched ahead of him, with the leader 10 yards away. Hayes grabbed the baton and barreled past five runners to win by five yards.

At the finish line Charles Walter, the assistant coach of the U.S. Olympic track-and-field team, looked at his stop watch. He looked at it again and shook his head. "This is ridiculous," Walter said. "I've got Hayes doing the last 100 in 8.6."

165

"It's ridiculous maybe," said head coach Bob Giegengack, "but it must be right. Hayes had to do the impossible to win as big as he did from so far back. Nobody ever was timed in 8.6 for 100 meters, but I have to believe that Bob Hayes did it."

But football was still Bob Hayes's favorite sport. He hurried home from Tokyo to rejoin the Florida A. & M. team. The previous year he had been drafted by both the Cowboys and the Denver Broncos of the American Football League as a "future" choice; he was eligible for the draft of college players because his original class was about to graduate although he still had a year of college eligibility left. At Florida A. & M. he was a running halfback, a flanker, a punter and place kicker. He also ran back kickoffs and punts. Selected to play in the North–South Game at Miami, he went 45 yards for a touchdown as a runner on an end-around play. He was selected as the game's Most Valuable Player. In the Senior Bowl, he caught a 45-yard touchdown pass from quarterback Joe Namath of Alabama.

Namath, who had signed a reported $400,000 contract with the New York Jets of the AFL, had good-naturedly needled Hayes in practice. In one drill Namath kept calling for long passes.

"No, no," Hayes said, "give me a short one. I

166

Using his world-record speed, Hayes sprints into
the end zone.

can't run that far any more. I like the short ones."

"If you're the world's fastest human," Namath replied, "then you can get out there for the long one."

"I'd have got more than $400,000 if I was a quarterback," Hayes said, "But I had to take $5 and a bicycle."

Hayes reportedly received a guarantee of $100,000 over three years from the Cowboys. But there was no way of knowing if he would earn it. No rookie is ever sure of making an NFL team. His college coach, Jake Gaither, thought he would make it. Gaither said, "Hayes is what a football player should be— agile, mobile and hostile. He's coachable, he accepts criticism, he doesn't smoke or drink. And he wants to win—that's what I mean about being hostile." Tom Landry, the head coach of the Cowboys, thought he'd make it, too. "Hayes is the first sprinter I've ever seen who is also a great football player," Landry said. "He not only has speed, he knows how to control it."

In his calmly confident manner, Bob Hayes thought he would make it, too. "I'm different than the other sprinters who tried to make the NFL," he said. "First, the others didn't play college football. They lost their football coordination. Maybe in high school they were good in both track and football, but if you don't stay with the game in college,

168

you lose what you had. Another thing, maybe they didn't have the heart to play in the NFL. Third, when most sprinters put on a football suit, they try to outrun everybody. They don't use their blockers. I've found that my speed rates about sixth in importance to me as a football player. The five things more important are five good blockers."

Hayes soon began to convince other people, too. In workouts for the East–West All-Star Game at Buffalo, New York, he impressed Paul (Bear) Bryant, the head coach at the University of Alabama. Bryant watched Hayes running pass patterns one day and told a bystander, "He's no straightaway sprinter. He's got moves and he can run all day. Football is easy for him. He's smart. He learns quickly, and you never saw anybody catch the ball like he does: over his shoulder, off his shoetops, anywhere. If it's close, he'll get it. And I don't think he ever had to catch the ball much. At Florida A. & M. they ran most of the time. Let's find out."

Bryant called Hayes aside and asked him where he had learned to catch the ball so well. "In the North–South Game and in the Senior Bowl," Hayes said. "Nobody threw to me much before."

Hayes caught four passes in the East–West Game and then moved on to the College All-Star training

169

camp. There he failed to impress the coaches. He dropped so many passes that it prompted the wise-crack that he had 9.1 feet and 12.1 hands. Against the NFL champion Cleveland Browns, he caught the first pass thrown to him for a 16-yard gain, but he was never thrown to again. When he reported to the Cowboys, he was a question mark. And he was so nervous that he was an easy target for the Cowboy veterans in the daily workouts.

"Coach," he complained one day to aide Red Hickey, "I can't get by that linebacker. He grabs me every time."

"That's the way it is in this game," Hickey replied. "They'll all try to hold you. You've got to learn to dodge him, fake him, anything, but you've got to get around him some way."

"But I can't do it," Hayes said.

"You'll do it or you'll be on your way home," Hickey said.

He soon learned to get by the linebacker and to hold onto his passes. Several weeks later Red Hickey said, "Talk about your great rookies—guys like Bobby Mitchell and Lenny Moore—Hayes is way ahead of them at the same stage. I've never seen a rookie with such potential. He reminds me a lot of Don Hutson, with his speed and great hands. But he's faster than Hutson. And he has moves,

170

Hayes catches a pass in the end zone for another Cowboy score.

he's tough, he's durable, he's teachable. What more can you ask?"

The week before the Cowboys were to open the 1965 season against the New York Giants, Hickey had a talk with Hayes. "Keep cool," Hickey advised him. "There's no reason to be nervous. You know all the plays. And you can execute them."

The Cowboys routed the Giants, 31–2, and Hayes caught two passes for 81 yards, including a 45-yard touchdown play. The next week, against the Washington Redskins, he caught a 46-yard touchdown pass and ran 11 yards for another touchdown on an end-around play in which he was used as a ball carrier. Another touchdown catch, a 23-yard play, was nullified by a penalty, but Hayes had sparked the Cowboys to a 27–7 victory. More important, he had convinced his teammates that he was a football player, not a track star.

In the locker room after the game one of the veterans announced, "The game ball goes to—Bob Hayes."

Several minutes later, Hayes stood in front of his locker, holding his prized game ball and accepting congratulations from newsmen.

"Great game," one of the sportswriters said.

"Great?" snorted a nearby teammate, veteran

172

defensive back Mike Gaechter. "He wasn't great. He was stupendous."

Barring injury, the word "stupendous" will be used to describe Bob Hayes for many years to come.

ABOUT THE AUTHOR

DAVE ANDERSON has covered professional football for many years as a sports writer for the New York *Journal-American*. He has written for the *Saturday Evening Post, True, Sports Illustrated* and *Sport* magazine. He is the author of the *Pro Football Handbook* and the *Major League Baseball Handbook* (Lowell Press) and received the 1965 E. P. Dutton Award for Best Sports Stories. He is also the author of *Great Quarterbacks of the NFL* (Punt, Pass and Kick Library #2).

Mr. Anderson lives in Tenafly, New Jersey, with his wife and four children.

Index

177

179

Photograph credits:
Vernon J. Biever, 61, 72, 78, 88, 102, 104, 150-151; Walter
Iooss, Jr., 83; Ken Regan, 2, 38, 56, 70, 93, 116-117; UPI,
6, 31, 34-35, 42-43, 46, 64-65, 77, 112, 115, 119, 122(right),
128, 132, 154, 164, 171; Wide World, ii, 15, 18, 20, 24, 53,
97, 109, 122(left), 134-135, 136, 140, 145, 156, 167.

OTHER BOOKS IN THE PUNT, PASS AND KICK LIBRARY

THE PUNT PASS AND KICK
LIBRARY
NFL